143 POEMS

GELU NICOLAE IONESCU

Gotham Books

30 N Gould St.
Ste. 20820, Sheridan, WY 82801

Phone: 1 (307) 464-7800

© 2023 *Gelu Nicolae Ionescu*. All rights reserved.

No part of this book may be reproduced, stored in a retrieval system, or transmitted by any means without the written permission of the author.

Published by Gotham Books (September 02, 2023)

ISBN: 979-8-88775-376-8 (P)
ISBN: 979-8-88775-377-5 (E)

Because of the dynamic nature of the Internet, any web addresses or links contained in this book may have changed since publication and may no longer be valid.

The views expressed in this work are solely those of the author and do not necessarily reflect the views of the publisher, and the publisher hereby disclaims any responsibility for them.

SORIN PETCULESCU
COVER PHOTO TAKEN BY:

TRANSLATORS:

CARMEN NEAGU & GELU NICOLAE IONESCU

TABLE OF CONTENTS

OCTOBER, SOMETIMES… 1

A MAGIC AUTUMN… 2

LETTER TO NOVEMBER 4

POETIC JOURNAL: NOVEMBER 9TH, 2022 5

HAPPY-WHO? 6

STORY FROM A LIFE 8

THE MORNING OF THE GODDESS...................................... 10

THE SPRING'S TRAIN STATION POET-A GIDDY BALLAD- 11

TRANSPARENT STRADIVARIUS MUSEUM 14

ST.VALENTINE, HOW CAN I FORGET ABOUT YOU?............. 16

THE STAKES OF DREAMING... 19

ABOUT YOU AND ABOUT SPRING, AT TWILIGHT 21

OTHER WORDS 23

FLOWERING ETERNITY… 24

BREAKING REFLECTIONS-2 25

THE SNOWFALL OF THE SNAILS-2...................................... 26

NO!.. 27

AFTER ONE YEAR 28

MAGNOLIAS ŞI MONGOLIAS-2.. 29

ETER LIKE A SILENCE OF SNOWS 30

ON GIVEN WORDS 31

NEWS	32
COFFEE POURED ON LONGING	33
SQUARED	34
I WOKE UP WITH DIFFERENT EYES!	35
AT THE BEACH	36
BARBU'S HOURGLASS	37
IN THE AFTERNOON GREAT FOR FLESH	38
THIS SUMMER PAINTING IS MOVING	39
NOT NAKED, BUT FILLED WITH LOVE!	41
HOW THE SUN ROSE IN THE FOURTH DAY…	42
AUTOPORTRET	43
DREAM	44
9 AND SOME	45
BARBARIC	46
THE CLOCK THAT STOPPED	47
THE JURNAL OF TIME TOO CLOSE	48
ON SHORES OF ALCOHOL ON SHORES OF ALCOVE	50
OFTEN DESTINY	52
WHAT DO YOU SAY, BEAUTIFUL?	53
ORPHEUS WHATEVER…	54
DIFFERENT KIND OF SEPTEMBER	55
COSMOGENY-2	56
TUMULT…	57
END OF SUMMER	58

Title	Page
AND THIS IS HOW I GREW UP JUST WHEN MY VANITY SHRANKED	59
HOW THE FACE OF THE THOUGHT COMES BACK	61
UNDER A TEA SHADOW	63
TODAY THE SNOWFALL SCREAMED AT ME WITH WHITE	64
RAIN WITH A DIFFERENT KIND OF SUN…	65
UN-REGRETS	66
HOMO VAMAIOTUS NEPLATONICUS	68
FROM A DRIZZLE – THE SEA FROM AN OWL – THE HORIZON…	69
JOYS	71
AT THE WELLS	72
SADNESS	74
18	75
SEAGULLS LIKE SOME DOGS OF THE SKY	76
MASS-MEDIA STILL HATES THE POETRY TODAY	78
TERRIBLE, NECESSARY AND ETERNAL PERVERSION	79
EVENING WAS YOUR DRESS	80
WINE	82
VIOLET, TODAY BE JUST VIOLET!	83
AN ANTIQUE AFTERNOON	85
AUTOPORTRET WITH WINTER	87
WINDOW	88
THE WINE OF THAT RAIN, OLD, TOO LATE…	89

AT ONE TIME, I LIVED NEXT TO THE MARKET PLACE	90
VISION	91
IT SNOWS ON NOTHING	92
SO WHAT?	93
MY SEA WAS CALLED: THE UNITED STATES OF THE BEAUTIFUL RAINS OF SUMMER	94
PINK IOANA	95
THE WOMAN PLAYING PIANO ON ME	96
MAY 13TH AT THE BEACH	97
POEM IN THREE TIMELINES	100
GODESS – ARCHIPELAGO OF FLESH AND DREAM	103
IF ONE DAY YOU'D BE MY SHEET OF PAPER	104
WHEN LOVE MEETS WORDS…	106
SILVER STOVE	108
JUST BE!	109
EVENING-FRAME AND BRAZILIAN SARA	110
THE ELEGY OF THE STARS	112
WINTER PAINTING WITH FIRE IN THE STOVE	114
CONFESSION	116
IN FACT…	117
REMEMBER IN THREE TIMELINES	118
LOST IN A GERBERA TRIANGLE	121
DNA OF THE SEAS	124
SHUT UP!	126

THE MOMENT TEMPLE	127
CRAZY EARTH	129
AND WHAT A POET WAS I WHEN "IS SNOWING!"- I RANTED!	131
REMEMBER IN THREE TIMELINES	133
FOR ELISE, WHERE ELISE IS NOT ELISE	135
TO BETTER ENTER THE HAPINESS WITHDRAWAL	139
WOMAN-ORANGE	140
RECITATIONS	141
THE ROAD TO YOU	142
A BOUQUET OF APPLE TREE FLOWERS	143
AB	145
DESCRIPTION OF FALLING IN LOVE	146
BUT WHAT IS RAIN? A SEA FOR AN HOUR – ION BARBU WOULD SAY, MAYBE..	148
A NOTHING OF PLATINUM	149
YOU SEE, LOVE IS LIKE TAKING CARE OF THE GRAPE VINE..	150
MASK	152
BOOMERANG OF BLUE -POETIC SYMPHONY	154
OF LOVE	157
THE MARCHING BAND OF STOLEN KISSES	158
LOVE	161
GOOD BYE	162
REWARD	163

THE DAWN IS A TRAIN	164
ALMOST WHITE, STILL BLUE	166
A HEAD TURN	167
SICK OF COMPARISONS	168
WHEN THE RAIN STOPPED	170
SUMMER	171
TODAY I FEEL LIKE CONFESSING	172
HYMN	173
CLEAR MOONSHINE IN THE NEIBORHOOD OF MIRRORS	174
EROS AND TANATHOS	176
WITH THE SPEED OF SILENCE	177
HELL	179
HEAVEN	180
MASKS	181
HAPPY SONG	182
A SWEET GOOD-BYE	185
LUNATIC	186
GENESIS OF A JULY RAIN	187
POOR BALANCE	189
CONFESSION	190
A MEMORY	192
LYRIC GAMES	193
THIS SOUL DOESN'T STOP TALKING...LOOK AT WHAT IT SAYS...	194

LETTER TO HER	195
THE FOOL WHO WAS WATCHING YOU…	196
FIRST ACT	198
STATE	199
PERIOD AND FROM THE BEGINNING	200
I WAS FALLING	201
LOST IN THE GEOMETRY OF YOUR SMILE	202
WHEN IT RAINS	203
BROKEN SILENCE	204
I WROTE ON THE PAPER OF THIS DAWN A POEM – 24 APRILIE 2023	205

OCTOBER, SOMETIMES...

I WILL REMEMBER, MAYBE, SOMEDAY,
THESE NIGHTS WHEN THE STARS ARE SLASHING AND PRICKING ME,
WHERE THE MOON IS HITTING ME LIKE AN IRON BALL ON MY SCRUFF...
AND, MAYBE, I WILL SMILE SAYING: IT IS LIFE!

THERE ARE MOMENTS WHEN THE PAIN KNOCKS YOU DOWN
AND EVEN IF YOU'D INHALE ALL THE AIR FROM THE UNIVERSE
AND THE TEARS YOU WOULD HAVE THEM TRANSFORMED IN LYRICS
THE EMPTINESS IN YOUR CHEST AND THE WHITE OF SADNESS, YOU COULD NEVER FILL...

CONTEMPLATING AT YOUR OWN SNOWFALLS
AND RAIN OF THORNS AND VIRTUAL SUNRAYS
MOTHER NATURE IS A FACE OF TERRIBLE GRIMACE
AND YOU'RE RENOVATING EVERYTHING THAT MEANT "HOME".

MECHANICAL MOVEMENTS, HUMBLE,
SOMETIMES, YOU COULD LOOK INSANE...
WHEN A TEAR I SEE IS WATERING THE ASHED LOOK
"HE'S NOT A ROBOT", THEY'RE SAYING,
HE IS SORROWFUL, POOR FOOL...

AND, SUDDENLY, THE MOST PAINFUL "I DON'T KNOW"
GETS YOU LOST IN A DESERT
ASKING YOURSELF WHAT "YOU" AND "I" REALLY MEANS
IF IT IS SAFE TO LOVE OR NOT...

A MAGIC AUTUMN...

The world is my entire window
Through which I stare at you
As in childhood, like I used to,
In those holy moments,
Watching the silent snowfalls.

Such a long and beautiful fall,
Like a child's hair,
Like a long ago read story,
But not that long to
Get to
Finally
Kiss you
On this earth,
Not only in a dream!

Silence is not when you say nothing!
It's the desert of the darkness,
It's a mountain with peaks in a skyless sky,
Smoldering muteness of eter.

Streets disappearing under falling leaves,
Rainbow born from the wound...
I had to learn to call you Madam,
In a magical autumn!

The world is my entire window
Shattered by sadness and by vain!
And I don't know what miracle to beg for:
To see you? To forget you? To hope?
On our deserted stage
A memory and a silence play mayhem...

What an unpraised uproar!
The director seems to be long gone!

How awful is to understand that you are not man,
When you fell in love up to the last atom!
That you can be mortal
Only if it kills you, hungry for longing,
Of twilight's dragon!

The catcher of your iris,
I am coming, today, with my hand emptied of yours,
To worship the beginnings, again,
In the springtime temple, barbarically lost.

LETTER TO NOVEMBER

It's quiet at the garden's table
And it seems like the dimmed light rains.
The notebook sheets
Blown softly by the autumn winds.

Look, November is by clouds intoxicated.
The same as this boy writing at this table.
To the one, being his star.
In sky of the skies, the earth transforms him!

Faded be the flowers of the lips- kisses and smiles.
Once upon a time
And one time
With the leaves.

He stares in a blank dismay, like the trees.
In the horizons where to build the snows the masons are coming...
In fact, he's not writing!
The words are flowing from his crushed soul!

November, please do something, really!
For the goofiest man you know!

Give him the spirit of one of your mornings.
To come out safe from all the prickles.
To wake up and to be joyful.
And all his sins to be forgotten!

POETIC JOURNAL: NOVEMBER 9TH, 2022

From your own shadow
Is of the twilight the horizon
And lost I get in it
Without your glance
... butterfly that has forgotten its color.

From your smile the moon.
From your eyes stars.
From your movements breeze.
From your silence
Night
In which I cannot longer dream.

So..
In this case
Please.
Turn off my world
With your eyelids. Goddess.
And make it dream of yours of an instant.
Like it was...

HAPPY-WHO?

I'd remain still
If I'd imagine you'll return!
And I walk into the world
With stains
Of lipstick
Turquoise and cyclam
From your kisses unkissed...

My own piano keys,
Bored of being touched only by the blind rains,
Are writing, awaken,
Your fingers
Torrentials...

Even if the happiness stands when no seats are available,
Don't get off from our sun's, blonde bus,
Because our time is measured by a fountain,
An hourglass of blues
And the squared driver
So tipsy
Oh God,
Can take us to Dubai!

For me, the time is measured
By the hourglass of your body
And is stealing my sand- like caresses
-To unpeel them, not a chance!-

The sticky stars
Are staying in our May's sky
A sonata quadrature
When I met you, like never before...
Could be imagination that I feel
And how I see you.

BUT WITHOUT ANY CALAMITY.
BONDAGE. KNOTS
AND THE SKY COULD BE MY EMPTY FHISHING NET...

I AM STOMPING MY FOOT
PAINTED
BY THE GRASS
BY THE STONE
BY THE HORIZON THAT SPRAINED BLINKS
AND I WRITE STUPID THINGS. RIGHT AWAY.
WHEN, LOOK!
HER NUDE IS WAITING FOR ME
TO UNDRESS HER COLORS
AND ITS WHOLE ART.
WHEN OTHER NUDES ARE SCOLDING ME
THAT I DON'T PAINT THEM.
I DON'T DREAM ABOUT THEM!
WHEN, LOOK...

STORY FROM A LIFE

Hypnotic her gaze was snowing
Once upon a time
And quiet and all of a sudden
With her
With the snowfall
Becoming right then
An another...

Hypnotic her gaze was snowing
Once upon a time
With the snowfall
Which all of a sudden
It wasn't of a winter at all
But more of a tolerant spring
Not arongant at all rather...

And all of a sudden
The daylight transformed into a sea
On which
I couldn't stand on my feet
From which
I can't get out without the wonder
And began to call it horizon
Only on its eyelashes

On the fine ice polished by the sun
The looks of young girls pass
You'd say they are all horizon
Softly sitting on its eyelashes

Is aproaching - and for how many times?!-
The night to the dreaming of the dream of its summer
When the stars will start walzing outside
Perfumed by the lilacs

Wearing serrated small vest on their top...

Covered by the winter of writing
Her flesh -snowfall of the love-
Will melt by sunrays
Risen by chresses and kiss
And waves of rain will fall
From the sky's sea
But I will keep it quiet
Beeing too damn personal

THE MORNING OF THE GODDESS

With a rain of coffee. What a long trailing morning.
With dreams transformed into a sugar cube. Right next to.
The neck wearing diamonds of the shooting stars.
Clasped by the timid sun's bright hand!
What a long trailing morning.
Long as a new life for it is to arrive.
Like two pageboys
Dizzy from the perfume of her rosy cheek's mirage!
In the coffee grounds lightly sifted.
The kiss was lifted
And settled
And an imense love. Larger than
Anything that it could be.
A love fallen like from Mars
Laughing with roars of the people and death!
What a long trailing morning.
With all his thoughts to catch.
To pick softly from her lips
With his lips a coffee drop.

THE SPRING'S TRAIN STATION POET ~A GIDDY BALLAD~

From de white of the snowfalls
To the white of the flower buds.
I will walk between two suns:
One with teeth and one with clouds.
Goddesses in love
From the snowdrops flowers born
I will rip them fast apart
To make them crooked
To leave their ankles to the wind.
Green wind, green earth.
For all the green to be seen.
The greenest madness!
From fairytale's Green King
Unremitting I will ask your hand for me
And I will crucify him on water.
Till he will agree!
The water that won't remember
When frozen it will suffer
The water that won't remember
What the rains teribbly sprinkles
Water lake and imense water
Everyone's water in tears
Water in wave, water in boots.
Drink water, everyone's beautiful water...
And through the new sun's eyelashes
I will stare at passing ladies
With the step of my heart
On my chest pressing hard...
New shaggy hopes
Will leave the house again.
From a green stumble

WILL FALL BACK IN LIFE ONCE MORE.
UPON THE HURT OF THE KNEES
WE'D GIVE THE NAME OF THE LOVE
ALSO TO THE ELBOWS AND THE TEMPLES
FOR NO DOCTOR REMAINS ABLE...
A HARD CORE STOP AT THE SEA SHORE
SHIPS ARE FALLING TO REMOTENESS
FALLING ARE EVEN THE STARS OF CHANGES
AT REFLUX JUST DAWN ARRIVES IN
SNOWS OVER THESE SEVEN HOUSES!
("SEVEN SNOWS REMAIN TO FALL"...)
WINTER REMAINS BE GONE
FOR LIGHT YEARS TO RETURN!
AND THE LOVES WHICH WILL NOT BE
BLOOMING BE'N ETERNITY
AND WILL SHAKE IT IN THE PAST
LIKE... REMAINDERS OF CONCEIT...
AND THE LOVES WHICH WILL NOT BE
BLOOMING THOUSANDS
THOUSANDS OF A NEW BORN STARS
FILL MY CUP WITH THREE RAIN POURS
CAUSE MY THIRST IS GETTING FULL.
IS NOT WINE NOR A WEAK MALT.
IS NO MOUTH TO DRINK IT ALL
FOR HOW BIG MY THIRST HAS GROWN!
AND FOR ALL THE LOVES THAT WERE NOT
THOUSANDS HERE IN BLOOM MAY BE...
FLOWERS LEMON FLOWERS ORANGE...
CRUSHING WITH BARE HAND A GLASS!
RAINS FROM THE CHEST POCKETS
OF THE INTELLIGENT SKY
AND THE RAIN WITHOUT UMBRELLA
AKWARD AND REBELLIOUS
TOO MUCH AS A SEASON'S EARDRUM.
LIKE A HALO EARDRUM, EVEN MORE
MAY THEY WET YOU TO THE BONE
GIFTING KISSES IN EXCHANGE OF
MAY THEIR WHOLENESS MAKE YOU WHOLE!
THIS SEASON TRAIN

...JUMP FROM IT AND IS NOT CHORUS
CAUSE YOUR KISSING OF TRAIN STATIONS
WHICH SOMETIMES THEY WAITED FOR...
VENTRILOQUIST POETRY
YOU DON'T STOP A BIT AT ALL
WHY YOU SAYING ALL THE THINGS
TO THE WORLD WHICH CANNOT TAKE
EITHER LONG OR EITHER WIDE!

TRANSPARENT STRADIVARIUS MUSEUM

ISN'T DARK! IT'S RAVEN!
MACABER DUST'S SOUL ON THE ROAD
BLIND THE WIND WILL BLOW IT
ISN'T DARK! IT'S RAVEN!
KEEP QUIET! PLAY THE SILENCE!
AT THE VIOLIN
OF BACOVIA!
WHOLE SCORES OF SIGHS...ONLY HER
THE VIOLIN
OF BACOVIA
VIOLIN
COULD
PLAY THEM...
SHE
A SONG HERSELF
SHE
THE SILENCE SPELL.
MONDAY...ONLY ANOTHER INVITATION TO THE ALWAYS
DANCE
IN THE DARKNESS GOD.
DARKNESS OF THE WEEK, IN THE WILDERNESS.
OF THE DEAD AND ALIVE OF THE DARKNESS...
MONDAY. WHAT A CROSS IS THE BOW ON THE VIOLIN!
THE SOUNDS THAT ARE TO DIE!
THE SOUNDS WITHOUT THE SUMMER!
LOOK HOW IT SPREADS
IN THE WINTER THE WILLOW TOWARD YOU
LIMBER OF CARESSES THAT CAN'T HOLD
OR LIKE IT COULD BELIEVE
THAT YOU COULD BE GREEN FOR IT...
ISN'T DARK! IT'S RAVEN!
THE SHIP OF BLACK ORT
FAILING IN THE DEAD CITY

That was never port
Till the arrival of the sea from the raven...
Hopes? Ha! How funny!
If it wouldn't be this valley of lamentation in me
Riots of laughts it would then be
The laughs to laugh of me...
Isn't dark! It's raven!
And this poem is not cake!
What a cross is the bow on the violin!
Of the sounds that are not to die!
The sounds without summer!
To whom you play don't listen anymore
And who's listening
Nobody plays for!

ST. VALENTINE, HOW CAN I FORGET ABOUT YOU?

Take it and read it!
As this poet celebrates!
13th-14th
What distemper to be seen
Just three words remembers he
And his dreams, up to the stars.
How can he forget them now?
This becomes a great big joke:
He has broken all his silence!
The first two of course you'd guess
Cause today it's a day...
But the third which one could be
You could never guess, you see!
He sits still just eyes are speaking
It could be a spell I'd say!
His lips are a stealth awaiting
For the kiss ready for thee.
One is saying like a mother:
"What is left for him to say,
When the crazy love he's feeling
Is the storm in chest that's brewing?"
Other saying: "Still good that he is writing,
But don't you think he writes to you!
The whole world would rose in seconds
If he'd make her happy"
Other saying, with concern:
"You're no doctor,
But if asking in a whim
Poor guy, what is wrong with him?
And you wonder how can be
So much love for one to be..."
And wham bam, here's now is now
Mother of the amber stone:

"Dark eyes, brown eyes,
Green eyes, blue?
What's the spell he's under now?"
Straight hair, wavy,
He's too way, too much in love,
Blonde, brown hair, or red hair, think?"
One of them cleverly smiling
You can tell it by the grimace:
"I'm afraid
You'll never know
Cause he didn't write it, he just blinds you,
So we won't see he's in love"
When another puzzled, asking
Curios and shriveling:
"But why doesn't he write clearly?
With his wondering own words?"
One is answering still smiling
With an emphasis and blinking:
"You small doctor, you can ask,
But he nothing will reveal!"
And another comes concluding
As she wants to feel important:
"This champagne of sweet poem,
Let's stay here a while and drink,
Maybe he will mention here
Who is she, the chosen girl!
Smiles and laughts if you give him,
More poems he'll bring again!
But with hope that he'd reveal
You will wait for years to hear!
From the Daci and Romans customs,
Many years have passed in time...
It will pass still many more
And his longing be unheard!
C'mon don't torment in vain!
Read the poem and be fair
And the world to find out whole
That the author is in love!
What is with the rest of story

Is no business for the reader!
We will maybe find out sometime
With a true patience and skill for!"

THE STAKES OF DREAMING

NOT STAYING ASIDE EITHER,
AT THE LIFE'S ALLOWED POKER GAME
I WANTED TO DRAW A SIGLE CARD:
THE QUEEN OF MY DREAM!
AND I AM AWAKENING DREAMING FROM A DREAM
A WONDERING SHIP
ON HER SEA OF TIME
ROWING TO BE FOR HER
ALWAYS
A SEASHORE-HUG...
AND HAVE LEFT ON MY SHOULDERS RUINS OF FORGOTTEN TEMPLES
AND IN MY EYES RUINS OF SPARKLES
AND ROMPING IN MY BIRDCAGE CHEST
A BIRD THAT KNOWS HOW TO SING...
AND AGAIN I NEED TO ARRIVE FUMBLING
AT THE TABLES WHERE THE CARDS ARE DEALT!
FOR MUCH I LOST, I LAUGH AND I CRY
AND I SAY IN MY MIND:
TO HER, THE ONE
THAT WILL GO TO THE BEACH
WHEN I WILL BE FOR HER SUMMER, SUN
THE STORY
TAUGHT ME, WITH THE ONCE UPON A TIME,
TO CALL HER THE FAIRY ILEANA COSANZEANA!
WITH HER
AT THE SEA SHORE, I'D DRINK EVERYTHING
AN ABSOLUT INFINIT COCKTAIL, AND NOT JUST A COFFEE!
AND YOUNG SEAGULLS MAY FLY OUR DESPAIRS
AND MAY TAKE THEM FAR AWAY
TO DROWN THE HATE AND BETRAYAL
WHERE THE SEA IS THE DEEPEST!
AND MAY GREEN TO WHITER

THE FALLS
AND MAY SHATTER OUR MIRRORS
THE FANTASIES!

ABOUT YOU AND ABOUT SPRING, AT TWILIGHT

...Then, light's flight
Of twilight.
Which makes everything rippen.
In the most hidden fair.
It's bought
With most admired dough
Of the sight...
With you it's a different story
Out of the world things happen
It wasn't! It is!
It wasn't a princess once upon a time! You are!
And swear that even your walking is a gift
To light up de stars. Not again.
Threading with you rare walk
A pavement breaker hidden inside the asphalt.
When coming, is like you're bringing a wave
And your soft walk is my desired sop
And you are the princess of the fire stars
That opens before me the castle of the hour of the crystal...
Along a pederost shore
Of a sea that never was.
Flying a lace like light
Flying watercolor zephyr...
Then, the flight of the light
Drenched by a groping rain
And in the air- flickering candle
I see your contour of your gape...
Hearing rejoycing of new whispers
Wind rejoycing of the new leaf
And the new leaf is shaking a bit, at first.

AND THE FLIGHT OF THE LIGHT WILL TAKE THEM TO NIGHT
AND THE FLIGHT OF THE LIGHT WILL TAKE THEM SOMEWHERE...
...THEN, THE FLIGHT OF THE LIGHT, AGAIN AND AGAIN IN A NON-CARDINAL ETER
TOO UNSETTLELING FOR STARS, TOO VAGABOND
THE FLIGHT OF THE LIGHT, A FLIGHT OR A SEA WAVE...

OTHER WORDS

-Don't get tired of cyclam!
Like no branch is tired of its leaves!
Don't get tired of cyclam!
-Even if my feelings, maybe,
Being entirely wild,
Could be porched sometime?
-Don't get tired of cyclam!
Like no branch is tired of its leaves!
Don't get tired of cyclam!
At lunch, it happened,
Instead of dreams, rain!
And that didn't bother me at all!
 -Don't ever get tired of cyclam!
Like no branch is tired of its leaves!
Don't get tired of cyclam!
-And it amazes me, sometimes, all of a sudden,
The motionless movement of things!
-Don't ever get tired of cyclam!
-When it rains I am in the north, it seems like...
-Don't ever get tired of cyclam!
-When the sunset light
Is gone ...
To mix with her big blue
The writting of a passing hand
And bitterly stars light up for me
To suffer while reading...
-Don't get tired of cyclam!
Like no branch is tired of its leaves!
Don't get tired of cyclam!

FLOWERING ETERNITY...

At first, there is, a silence.
How it hasn't snowed in a long time
From souls and minds...
Then it shoots guns of rain in the wind,
Shooting the green, the blue, the earth;
Shooting the angel and demon,
Of grief, and longing.
Dizzyingly piercing us!
Is getting late way too soon.
Flowing blue, defying time,
A moon that I don't know is rising.
New breast in the palm of the gaze,
Like a glimpse of love...
Crazy crickets searching for ephemeral songs
Among the blooms always too early bloomed,
On a strange springtime
That doesn't want to become summer ...
But just to be cold, to shudder
Beautifully, the flattened dumpling of your tighs...

BREAKING REFLECTIONS-2

I WILL NEVER ASK MYSELF ALL THE TIME
WHO BROKE THE CASTLE WINDOWS FROM MY THOUGHTS?
AND WHO BROKE THE TANGO WITHOUT MUSIC
AND WHO BROKE THE OLD REFLECTIONS
ENTERING IN ITS SOUL THEIR SHARDS OF GLASS...
EPIC SECOND,
IN WHICH I LISTEN TO YOU
HOW YOU DON'T PLAY PIANO ANYMORE...
PIANO QUIETNESS...
THEN,
WINDOW SILL UNDER THE RAIN ARE PIANO KEYS UNDER YOUR FINGERS
PLAYING THE HAPINESS LIKE
PLAYING LIKE DREAMING
IN A DRESS LIKE A SLIDE...
HOW MY GAZE WAS SNOWING
OVER YOU!
NAKED BACK, AND STRAIGHT AND OPAQUE
LIKE A TWILIGHT
THAT DOESN'T FALL NOR INTO A DAWN
NOR INTO A NIGHT.
YOU WERE PLAYING HAPPINESS IT SEEMED LIKE
TODAY
I AM WATCHING MYSELF IN A SONG
SOUNDFUL MIRROR...ITSELF BROKEN ...
AND IN THE END WHO SHATTERED THE WINDOWS OF THE OLD CASTLE
AND WHO BROKE THE TANGO
AND WALKED IN HERE, AND STILL WALKS
IN THE ETERNAL EPIC SECOND?

THE SNOWFALL OF THE SNAILS-2

They walk like they are chewing earth...
Chewing its infinity
Like a chewing gum
As if, that only on them can fully snow...
Slowly...
Too slow!
They walk as if they are telling
The story of each millimeter of the road.

Intangible house of rain
-Who and how to rain the rain?-
Falling apart under the thunder of your own gaze...
Shadow of a giant lily...
The air of this house
Whose misteriously opened windows
Will make it seem like a flute
To where the lavender, the zephyr and oriental aromas sing ...

The snail's snow is not melting far away
But near, in the eyes!
To the feather of the smoothed gaze.

The snowfall revealed like a bread from the oven
Of the poles
And offered on the drummer's table
From, the Vax Albina, the unestablished music band!
Hit them daddy, this is it!
Courage, man!
My hearing has rubber earplugs of a "Again, man?"
The winter earplugs
Are burnt by the scorching heat!...

NO!

I am not watching today at your quiet window!
It's broken from a past love!
It was a skating rink of leavened noon days,
In the childhood with the skates of the
blossoming orchard...

It was, a long time ago, a blue confectionery- the
evening.
Where I would go get your kiss
And that taste
Was plowing
My soul...

The brick wall between day and night
Was demolished!
The evening remained like a ruin!
Visited by other lovers.

I retire alone, on a plain field,
In a brace of an autumn wind,
In a Madam,
To chew the apple bite of great grand father
Adam.

Belly-dancer this afternoon!
With long dresses like a gipsy
Another Fall will print better
With Luchian's point...

I write something
With my gaze
A letter
That will be lost right away in the horizon

AFTER ONE YEAR

White fled from the appletree flower
To play instant winters...
Like nano tangoes...

Blue as a state capital
To receive it on an evening
In a van
After one year...

Today, an empty jam bowl of a day...

A fleeing or a soar
But from what
And to where
Maybe some jam would bare...

The red sunset...Starlet
Carmine...Carmina!
Yes
Was that your name?

No! I don't want us to visit the sunset anymore!

MAGNOLIAS ȘI MONGOLIAS-2

IT FEELS LIKE SPRINGTIME TO ME, I THINK!
AND A RIOT OF LAUGHS INSTEAD OF A SKY

I'M BITTING HER TIGH OF SENSE

AFTER SO MUCH PATIENCE,
APPEARED, FINALLY, MAGNOLIA...

ETER LIKE A SILENCE OF SNOWS

AND IT STARTED!
THAT'S IT!
IT STARTED!
IT STARTED!

IT STARTED TO NOT SNOW ANY (MORE)...

ON GIVEN WORDS

Your bare sole
Like a once upon a time
Me, grass

NEWS

THE NEWEST CHECKMATE
THE NEWEST SNOWFALL
OF THE QUEEN OF WHITE
THE NEWEST NIGHT OF THE KING OF BLACK
WASTED EYELASHES OF PAWNS
MELT OF THE SUGAR WINDOWS
OPEN, PLEASE, A YARD TOWARDS SEASIDE!
TO VISIT WITH ME IN ONE WAVE
MY LOVER WEARING ONLY A SHAWL...

COFFEE POURED ON LONGING

Immanence, imminent stain
Coffee on a longing poured...
Is not gonna go away you said, but only if forgotten!

Coffee from nothing life
And still, bitter.

SQUARED

Welcome to the Buenos Aires's rain!

The paper airplanes
Taken off in childhood
Landed on the melancholy sunset

And...
I, like thinking of myself
Ran away from the hopscotch...

I WOKE UP WITH DIFFERENT EYES!

I want to kned you, dough that you are!
To rise you,
To bake you
To feed on you
And then to
Drink summer rains
What a wine!

AT THE BEACH

Evening- a wild mare
Was saddled
The blue hoofs
Running burning stone by stone
Wave by wave.

BARBU'S HOURGLASS

Flowing from Barbu's hourglass
Like from the eave of the world's idiocy

He has an hourglass
That can measure eternity.
Because the Imperial Iris
Is not gonna come
Not even in a billion's grain of fallen
sand.

IN THE AFTERNOON
GREAT FOR FLESH

SHE IS THE SHEET OF PAPER
THAT SLAPPED ME
WHEN I WROTE ON...

JUST WHEN
A HIDDEN FOUNTAIN
HAD FINISHED REPAIRING
THE TWILIGHT'S ARTESIAN...

WE TATTOOED OUR HANDS CLASP
FROM THE BOTTOM OF OUR FEET TO THE LATEST LATE
AND FROM LATE TO THE ECSTASY

OF SUMMER!
YES!
OF THE AFTERNOON SUMMER!

THIS SUMMER PAINTING IS MOVING

This summer painting is moving
Tied to a ship...to air
To a kite
To a walz
Of breeze
From fairies afternoons
And I have, today,
All the sea breeze
Tether to a smile.

This summer painting is moving
From all the flowers, from all its wrists of colors
From the red of the cheeks
From the watchful black eye
From the wanderer, vagabond rainbow,
From the cabaret of colors
Moving from blue to indigo
From yellow to ocher

This summer painting is moving
Especially with each breath that I take
And I show up
With the elbows of thoughts resting on flowers of blooms
And blossoms
And flights of nights
To take a look at the abyss
Only...
Only to be born-who knows?- a star
From my gaze...
Twilight's blue rose
I will brake it and I will give it to you as a tip

To not make me fail at love class
To not leave me alone somewhere anymore!

This summer painting is moving
And talking
And if I'd say that my soul is a bag
Filled with love for you
You don't ask me why!
It's like you'd want to search feelings identity
And
The feelings have no... identity card!

This summer painting
With frame of silence
Continues the detention of its border in a circle...

NOT NAKED, BUT FILLED WITH LOVE!

Your good old man
Surprised you
With me even in your thoughts!
Not naked, but filled with love!
Not in silence,
But in rustle of silk
Not just in fact,
But as an idea of graffiti,
And like an erotical mania...
Dazzling crystal of a sunny day of love.
Only when I bit you harder you startled
No! You were not nectarine
Like I started to think
Smacking my lips dreamly...
Hungry for love...
I settled my twilight
Like a hat
And I move the horse
With chess
On a field...
To give a checkmate to the distances...
And when he will get tired,
I will tether him
To an orchid
To an idea...

HOW THE SUN ROSE IN THE FOURTH DAY...

POETIC... SWITCH?
DOES EXIST?
I AM PUTTING OUT THE POETRY!
I LIGHT IT UP...
A KIND OF SUN
AFTER THE FORTH DAY
    -AFTER I DON'T KNOW WHAT!-
RISING...

AUTOPORTRET

About me in the horizon
A question is speaking:
—Will other sunsets be able too
To lay you down for me like a peach?

Invariable questions without sky
Without canons.
Mister!

DREAM

It wasn't your name
This is how you were
I wouldn't be crazy to say it like this

Yesterday, the sea started with a song
And would end with the image of a delphin

Today starts with a kiss
And it doesn't end...the sea...
So just today I got to it for the first time...

9 AND SOME...

ON THE DESERTED BEACH
MY EYES MADE STONES AND SAND
LIKE KIDNEYS

IF YOU WOULD SHOW UP,
MY EYES WOULD MAKE SEA
LIKE NOTHING AND NOBODY
COULDN'T MAKE...

BARBARIC

TO HIM NOTHING WILL RESPOND BUT THE GREEN OF THE GRASS
AND THE BUCKS WILL BRING IN HIS HORNS THE MOON

HIS PAGANINI IS THE WIND FROM THE STEPPE
AND THE STARS RISE FOR IT IN A PIROUETTE

WILL SPEED UP
THROUGHOUT THE DAWN

ON A POET- HORSE
ON A CHECKMATE HORSE

AN INSANE
OF THE DISTANCES
EXILED

HE WILL BRAKE THE CANOPIES OF THE DRY WINE
WHERE ONLY THE GODS PARTY

AND WILL UNWED QUEENS
WITHOUT LEARNING TO ASK WHO...

THE CLOCK THAT STOPPED

A CLOCK OF COLORS STOPPED
ON THE ICONOSTASIS OF THE WONDER

THE JURNAL OF TIME TOO CLOSE

On this evening, the sky is closer to earth
Like the skin is to the clothes
And it seems it would build itself,
On the horizon's slab,
In the air next to the irises,
In the air next to the roses,
A train station where the angels get off
A train station of unhappened holidays...
A train station where the angels get off...

I catch myself to the twilight's walz
On the music of the Monalisa's silence!
And I dance the past!
And all the waters are running towards the sky

...
At the round arm of the moon
Dissapearing in a square
And in a hopscotch square
Unseen by you
And you and them!

This evening, the sky is closer to earth
And still aproaching it
Aproaching like a deer
It's aproaching:
Of his hand of poplar leaves
Of his hand of grape leaves
Of his hand of fresh furrow, fermented...
And will kiss it with rain
And will touch it with the wet snout of a deer...

Deer that ate my day
And it was a strong wind and it was cloak

AND IT WAS SUN
AND IT WAS WAX
AND IT WAS SNOUT OF RAIN
PULLING THE SUNSET CLOSER TO THE EARTH
PULLING IT FROM THE NIGHT'S DEEP WELL
WITH A BUCKET SINCE WHEN
BOUND TO THE FINE THROAT LIKE AN ETER

ON SHORES OF ALCOHOL
ON SHORES OF ALCOVE

ON SHORES OF ALCOHOL
ON SHORES OF ALCOVE
THE SUNSET WAS SNOWING
TOO HEAVY
WAY TOO HEAVY!
USELESS CRYING
THE WILLOWS
UNDERNEATH HER
RUNNING WERE THE CREATURES ARRIVED TO DRINK

ON SHORES OF ALCOHOL
ON SHORES OF ALCOVE
THE WIND FISHERMEN SHARPENS
THEY CAUGHT SALMON STRETCHED ON THE GROUND
THE NIGHT SNARE CAUGHT THEM SINGING
THE PASSING
RUNNING WERE THE CREATURES ARRIVED TO DRINK

ON SHORES OF ALCOHOL
ON SHORES OF ALCOVE
YOU THOUGHT THAT YOU'D FORGET
THAT YOU'D FORGIVE
THE CLUMSINESS OF THE RAIN
THE SUGGESTION OF THE CLOUDS
BIOTECHNOLOGY OF THE DAWN
FROM WERE WE TOO FELL

ON SHORES OF ALCOHOL
ON SHORES OF ALCOVE
WE WATCHED THE TALL MINES
THE MINES FROM THE HORIZONS
SOLAR MINES OF GOLD

GOLD OF AIR
EXTRACTED FROM GODS BREATHING
EXTRACTED FROM AFRODITA'S LOOKS.
FROM HELEN'S GAZE...

ON SHORES OF ALCOHOL
ON SHORES OF ALCOVE
BREATHING AND WATCHING
PRECIOUS AIR- SOLAR AIR
HIGH AIR. RING ON UNIVERSE'S FINGER
BUILDING VENICES OF RAINS
HUNTING NAKED
ME ZEN- YOU FAIRY

ON SHORES OF ALCOHOL
ON SHORES OF ALCOVE.
STICKING BAND-AIDS ON ACHILE'S HEEL
BOTH UNSTUCK FROM DESTINY...

OFTEN DESTINY

Often destiny to see each other
Especially like Narcissus in waters!
Often destiny
Hugs to stiffen

The evening is printing for me
The face
With -blue

Red blood of Eve
Flowing from a sunset
Of an exentric printer

Mixed with gin,
Mixed with fate...
You asking without asking
A cocktail of yesterday

WHAT DO YOU SAY, BEAUTIFUL?

I want to go to the whisky neighborhood
Of your city

You to walk on highheels on the grass of my sunsets

In the shadow of blooming linden tree
Changing my shadow

To bluntly love
All the way to the blood of time
Which yet didn't pass

Don't bite the hand that feeds you
With dreams
Of the poet
That today
With you
Makes acquintance

The mad dog barks roses
Without me

The lights would go off drowned in sunsets
Stripped of reeds

Of Danubes
Of seas
Stripped of rains
Don't ask me
But later on...

ORPHEUS WHATEVER...

Strange object, in the beginning, the woman!
She stays on your retina- framed by your eyelids
Not on a chair, but on the smile.
Not minutes! Days in a row
Months, years...
Until the time gets stripped of time...

Then, once taken in the feelings space
Of your mind
Under the roof of your affection,
The yesterday's object
starts moving...to move you
To be the same as any other people
With shadows and desires
Gestures, attitudes, kisses, caresses...
Awaking unsuspected pleasures
Any redoubt
Fallen down!
And she is moving inside your soul
In your mind, bothered by some of your moves

And walks limping, as if
Her ankle was sprained by your gaze!
And walks with her head down, and walks hurt
As if she lives with Beelzebub!

If the adolescence would be rain,
Women would be the mushrooms coming out after it...
To fill up, it seems like,
The boards of the future museums of natural and unnatural science

DIFFERENT KIND OF SEPTEMBER

I FAILED AGAIN THE PRESELECTION FOR THE RAIN CHORUS
FOR THE DRY LEAVES CHORUS
FOR THE WELDED WINDOW SILLS CHORUS
AND IT WILL RAIN AGAIN WITHOUT ME...
AND THE DRY LEAVES WILL FALL AGAIN WITHOUT ME
AND THE WINDOW SILLS WILL RING AGAIN WITHOUT ME...
DON'T SCOLD ME THAT I AM ABSENT
DON'T ASK ME WHERE MY THOUGHTS ARE
I FAILED AGAIN THE PRESELECTION FOR THE RAIN CHORUS
FOR THE DRY LEAVES CHORUS
FOR THE WELDED WINDOW SILLS CHORUS
I AM LOCKED OUTSIDE
IN THIS AUTUMN AIR, HUMID,
BY THE MOUTH OF A SEA KISSED LIKE
AS IF I'M SITTING ON A WRITING BENCH
AS IF I'M BREATHING A PARTICIPATION DIPLOMA

I WILL INVENT A RAIN BAG
TO PULL THE FISH FROM THE RAIN!
I AM SURE THAT RAIN HAS ITS OWN FISH, LIKE ANY OTHER WATER!
NOBODY PULL THEM OUT TILL NOW!
CAN YOU IMAGINE HOW BIG THEY MUST BE?
TO FISH IN THE RAIN! HOW STUPID, OR HOW BEAUTIFUL!
TO SEARCH FOR THE RAIN'S SHINE, TO SEARCH FOR A BOAT TO FLOAT ON THE RAIN
OR TO INVENT THEM, IF THEY WEREN'T ALREADY...

BOHEME! YOU TWIST ME LIKE A MUSTACHE LIKE A CURL
AND ONLY IF I'D BE A CURL OF TWILIGHT
TO LAY ON YOUR FACE
BLUE AS A QUESTION

COSMOGENY-2

In the morning light,
You are the morning's light...
You lie down and the light spreads over you
Both lazy and very beautiful
Inseparable even by the blinking of my eyelids
Or the sunset's eyelids.
And just like that my Universe is born
Of a seduced man
In the seventh instant
Since you walked through the door...

TUMULT...

I am unwinding in a writing
Like the snowfalls unwind.
Like the spine of a giant getting up unwinds.
Like the unfinished column of Brancusi unwinds.
Always going up towards the sky.
Up and up.
I am unwinding writing for you
Like the old crocheted vests
Of grandma's unwind.
Which can only warm only the soul, today.
Dressing my gaze.
I am unwinding on a writing for you
Lost in a metropolis.
On a busy street, but beautiful and happy
Like a cherry branch in April.

When you left
A rainbow appeared behind you
Like you were a summer rain
And I watched until it was hidding in blue
And I watched you leaving in the blue dress...

END OF SUMMER

It ended like a show, the summer!
But nobody applauds.
However, it was a successful comedy!

Behind the scenes of the sunny shores we are changing.
The sad civility of Fall will follow.
The make-up of the smiles washed by the cold rains
Slapping!

We hardly part from the costumes of the play with sun
Where we played the role of lovers, the happy ones,
The spoiled ones of the Universe...

We don't care to love anymore! We don't travel...
We don't laugh inside ourselves and in the sun!
Even the algae wither, dry and fall like leaves on the sidewalk.
Sometime all this solitude of the sadness it was a sunny sea

It ended like a show, the summer!
But nobody applauds.
However, it was a successful comedy!

AND THIS IS HOW I GREW UP JUST WHEN MY VANITY SHRANKED

I WAS TRAVELING
OR IT SEEM TO ME I WAS
WITH OR WITHOUT TICKET
BORN OR UNBORN
MAN
OR NOT A MAN!
TRAVELING!
CLIMBING EVERY DAY ON A MOUNTAIN OF TIME
WHAT IN THE FALL IT SEEMED TO ME LIKE A WALL
OF CLAY
OF LEAD!
CLIMBING ON A MOUNTAIN OF TIME ALWAYS ERODED BY
THE PAST
AND THERE WAS LESS AND LESS CLAY
WHEN I WAS LOVING.
WHEN I WAS CLIMBING...
THERE WAS LESS AND LESS CLAY!
AND I GOT OUT IN THE FIELD
TO BE WOOLF
AND I GOT OUT TO THE SEA
TO BE LIKE HER. ENDLESS...

THEN, EVERY DAY A MOUNTAIN OF TIME LIFTED ME INTO
THE FIELD
AND EVERY DAY A WAVE LIFTED ME TO THE SEA!
FOR A LONG TIME I WAS SEARCHING FOR THE ECHO OF AN
"I LOVE YOU"!
THE VERY FIRST DREAM WITH HER
IRREPEATABLE BLINKING
IRREPEATABLE MEETING
OF MY EYELIDS WITH A DREAM...

My safic lover,
Crossed legged,
Like a folded paper
On which old algoritms
Were sleeping in a toned down blue...
The journey of my looks
Towards her skin
That I have started from the dawn of me!
And I grew up just only when my vanity shrank

HOW THE FACE OF THE THOUGHT COMES BACK

Yesterday, I was squeezing the words
Crushed them like grapes
Yesterday, I was drinking the sweet grape juice
Of the words of the beginnings

Yesterday, after my first love,
I picked the vine of the words
Yesterday, after my first sadness,
I picked the vine of the words

They were just right
Rippen in an autumn of meanings
Under a sky painted by the flight of the cranes...
In sunsets like some blue sneezes...

Today, after an eternity
Passed without any pomp
And croched from blinks
 ~Double line stitch
One eye laughing
One eye crying~
The grape juice of the words of the beginnings
Became wine
And I am drunk of all
And I am shaking
Like I'm snowing
Like snowflakes in freezing sunsets
On forgotten pavements
That hurt me
This snowfall
Of mine
With me
The eternity will melt as well

AS THE SNOWFALLS MELT
AS THE FLOWERS MELT
AS THE SMILES MELT
AT THE TRAINS WINDOWS

A CRAZY NIGHT WILL COME
LIKE A RUNAWAY FROM THE HOSPICE OF A LOST TIME
AND IT WILL SET IN THIS LIVINGROOM MAYBE
A CONCERT PIANO
AND A NEW PERSON WILL PLAY IT
WITHOUT KNOWING WHAT IT WAS BEFORE

AND NONE OF THE PIANO KEYS WILL SOUND SAD
NO BREEZE ON THE DRAPES
AND I WILL WRITE
LIKE FROM A SNOWFALL
SHOWED UP FROM AFAR
A PIANO
WITH A FISH TAIL
WITH A SNAKE TAIL
WITH A SEA TAIL!
A PIANO PULLED BY SEVEN WHITE HORSES
LIKE A SLED FILLED WITH CHILDREN

THE PIANO WILL MELT TOO
AND EVERYTHING WILL BECOME WHITE
OR BLUE
OR RED
OR ANOTHER HUE
THE COLORS WILL MELT TOO
ANY CONTRASTS WILL MELT
ANY OPPOSITE DIRECTION
ANY NONSENSE
ALL WILL MELT!
AND THE PRINTING OF THE MELT WILL OPEN NEW
EXHIBITIONS

UNDER A TEA SHADOW

Let's kiss the Fall
Let's allow ourselves to be kissed!
To walk without umbrellas
On the streets
Under the arcades of waters escaped from seas
Ran away from the seashores
And from the swim
To kiss the Fall
To let ourselves be kissed
To walk without umbrellas...
To get soaking wet
Winds wearthed from North to blow
And to get a cold
To get a cold with love
Crazyness to sneeze us

TODAY THE SNOWFALL SCREAMED AT ME WITH WHITE

Today the snowfall screamed at me with white
And the only thing that got startled
Was a deer
Lost of a field and of woods
In my blood
Today the snowfall screamed at me with white
And the only thing that got startled
Was just a hare
Lost to other rabitts
It was a smile
Lost to other smiles
The snowfall screamed at me with white
And the only thing that got startled
I was You!

RAIN WITH A DIFFERENT KIND OF SUN...

It's a rain like a disheveled sea!
Scrambling with elbows
Between dry leaves
And it comes!
It's a rain about you
And it's saying good things...
It's a rain like a disheveled sea
About a beautiful lost Eve...

And singing are the troubadours of metal and tile
And playing are the drops at the piano and at the rust
And singing are the roosters on the roofs
Sharpen me the distance to kill them...

The red sunsets of the summers were thrown up in the air!
It's a perfumed rain, with petals,
As if is bathing this field in love with the sky
And I want to let a horizon to kiss me...

I drink the rain's juice
Made from remote distances freshly picked and crushed
Mixed with the sunset's grapes...
While they still didn't start to ferment
Longings, attitudes, desires...

Is the hour of different drunkness
And I drink blue, exactly like it,
I drink spring water
And I drink kisses and longing

UN-REGRETS

I don't regret the sunset in which we lost our kiss
Shattering by the hand of our soul
And fleeing into the world to be forgotten...

I don't regret the sunset
When our embrace got fractured...

I don't regret the end of the love poem written on your body
And the final period I placed on your ankle...

I don't regret the kisses what today stand as melted snows...
Neither the burnt candle that yesterday perfumed our room...

I don't regret either that we broke up badly
We loved each other too much to remain friends now
I don't miss you
I don't want to see you
I don't want to embrace you, to kiss you

I don't care with who you are now
If you are happy or not
Where you are
I don't want to know anything

When I randomly see you
I don't even smile, nor do I get sad
Nor I stay, nor I dance

And this poem I write
On a given subject

DENYING IT
BECAUSE I DON'T HAVE REGRETS FOR WHAT I AM
BECAUSE I AM
BECAUSE I LIVED
I LOVED
AND I FORGOT
AND
I AM HAPPY NOW, LIKE I WAS THEN
BECAUSE WRITTING AND LOVING IS MY LIFE

HOMO VAMAIOTUS NEPLATONICUS

WE WERE NAKED
AND THE SEA WAS WATCHING US
IN THE EYES
WITH HER WIDE OPEN ENDLESSNESS, BLUE,
OR GREEN, OR ...NEVERMIND...
DAWN APROACHING LIKE A FISHERMAN
WITH A NET
BLUE, OR GREEN , OR...NEVERMIND...

THE EVENING HYPHEN'S ROLE WAS
NOT TO BREAK APART OUR MEMORIES
IN SYLLABES
SO OUR SOUL- ALWAYS A CHILD-
WOULD BE ABLE TO SAY THEM
EVERY SINGLE TIME
WHILE LONGING FOR BEAUTY...

WE WERE NAKED
AND THE SEA WAS WATCHING US
INDISCRET
THROUGH A CREVICE OF THE HORIZON...
LURKING WITH HER STORMS
TO STEAL OUR KISSES
AND TAKE THEM FAR AWAY

FROM A DRIZZLE – THE SEA FROM AN OWL – THE HORIZON...

WAITING FOR THE SUNSET
IN A TRAIN STATION BUILT FROM US
AND WE'RE WAITING
TO FINISH FOR THE SKY TO TAILOR
A BLUE SHIRT
FROM THE BREEZE'S SILK
WHICH WAS LURKING FOR OUR TENDERNESS

I WAS LISTENING HOW THE SOUNDS SETTLED ON THINGS
LIKE A SNOW
AND ON THE BODIES FISHED FROM THE DEPTHS
ALWAYS UNKNOWN...
GATHERED AND MULTIPLIED FROM TOILETS
IN BROWN AND IN CHECKERS
HIDDEN IN THE REEDS AMONG INDISCREET FROGS...
BLUE TATTOOS THE CLOCKS WERE TICKING!

I WAS HAND IN HAND WITH THE ROSY MISS
WHO WAS TALKING TO ME
ABOUT THEOLOGY
AND THE SEA WAS HUMMING
AND SHE WAS TALKING...

I PUT ON THE BLUE SHIRT OF THE EVENING
INSCRIBED WITH THE LAST SUN RAYS
RAN AWAY FROM THE TROPICS TO THE TOPICS...
AND WITH A RAINBOW FALLEN INTO THE SEA...
I STARTED TO SWIM INTO THE NIGHT...

AS FOR AUTUMN, NOW I WANT HOAR
TO KISS ONE HAND OF YOURS!

PRESSING
LONGING
LIKE ON A PEDAL
ACCELERATING THE MORTALS PLEASURE...

JOYS

My neighbor from the 7th floor floods me with
wine
White
And I am sipping it from the white walls, from
underneath her shadow
More beautiful than the sunset's walk

My neighbor from the 7th floor floods me with
wine
And I always coming quicker
To grab her waist
Her breasts and her soul and her heels

When I will be hated by everyone here
She won't hate me at all!
My neighbor from the 7th floor she loves me in
the block!

AT THE WELLS

WHAT A WONDER!
THE WELLS WERE EVEN IN THE AIR,
NOT ONLY ON EARTH!
WHAT A WONDER!
WERE WELLS OF THE AIR IN THOSE SUNSETS
FROM THEM I WAS TAKING HEALTHIER BREATHS
RICHER, MORE NOURISHING!
WHAT A WONDER!
WERE WELLS OF THE AIR THOSE SUNSETS
TO DRINK FROM THEM FOR HOW THIRSTY FOR LOVE WE
WERE
FOR KISS
FOR CARESSES
FOR ADVENTURE! HOW MUCH THIRST?
WERE WELLS OF THE AIR IN THOSE SUNSETS
AND WE WERE TAKING OUT OF THEM MOUTHS OF HEAVEN
WERE WELLS OF THE AIR IN THOSE SUNSETS...
AND WHEN WE WERE EMPTIED THEM TOO THIRSTY
TOO MANY
THEY WERE FILLED BY A HORN
BY A VIOLIN
BY A FLUTE
BY A LONGING...

SEARCH! SEARCH FOR THE WELLS OF THE AIR EVEN IN
THESE SUNSETS!
AMONG BLUE WOODEN CHIPS
ON PEW BOARDS
AMONG EMERALDS AND EYES!
DON'T LET THEM FEEL ABANDONED BY WHAT'S ALIVE!
DON'T LEAVE THEM BE UNDRUNK!

FROM THEM TO GET KISSES
CARESSES

BE CAREFUL! DON'T DISTURB THEM!
PULL UP CAREFULLY THE FULL BUCKETS
PUSH DOWN SLOWLY THE EMPTY BUCKETS
AND PULL THEM UP CLEAR, FULL MOON FILLED

FROM FINE PEN- IN THE EVENING, TODAY,
AND TOMORROW FROM AN EGRET'S FEATHER
ON A SHEET OF PAPER
ON A SHEET OF MILK
ON A SHEET OF SNOW
ON A SHEET OF CHEEK
ON A SHEET OF BREAST...
ON A SHEET OF TEMPLE
ON A SHEET OF KISS
TIME WRITTING UNDER THE GLASS CEILING
OF A TUMULTOUS DESTINY.
EVEN ESOTERIC, SOMETIMES...
WHEN FROM SINE AND COSINE
SNEEZES AND FORMULAE DROP
OF FORGOTTEN PROBLEMS AND RAINS.

AND...WHAT A WONDER!- ANOTHER!
TODAY.
THE HORIZON SINE WAS SNEEZING BUTTERFLIES...
SNEEZING IRISES GARDENS...
SNEEZING PAST LOVES
FORGOTTEN KISSES IN RAINS AND SNOWFALLS...
NOW.
TO LEAVE IT ALONE OR TO FLIRT WITH?
THIS IS THE QUESTION!

SADNESS

It's sad!
It's autumn
And I was expelled from the sea's highschool!
Day and night classes
On a shore without time
With Plato and Aristotle
And Archimedes and Socrates...
With a school yard: Olimpus!

It's sad! It's autumn! It's a lot!
And the old bench broke!
The sand from inside the class
With ceiling of sky
It's now a lagoon of cold rains
And dry
Without fish, without ships
Just empty streams
Ran away from sea...

It's sad, it's autumn, it's a lot
And is mute!
I collect seashells, I subtract them, I multiply
them, permutate them...
To keep me company
To fill my palm's cup
In which I lifted the caresses of your body...

18

At 18, the time is giving you change...the eternity...
Of dreams...small change, to have some to spend!
At 18,
Your time is putting on makeup
What a summer evenings
And with
And wearing a sun with a tail
And making from each window
A small skating rink
For the gaze of crazy lovers!
The human iris to make pirouettes,
To make rains, the human tears...

At 18, time slaps you on your butt
On your tighs
On your face
And is pulling from you the queue you're sitting at
To catch a dream becaming true...

SEAGULLS LIKE SOME DOGS OF THE SKY

Is wondering miss Tanta, granny is wondering
What are the seagulls from the sea doing here with us?
Look! Seagulls in the neighborhood, in the fields!
Or sky's stray dogs could they be?

Entering through the door the Evening- a good neighbor of ours
Stepping on the Sun's yard a freshly cut blue grass.
And the seagulls screaming to the hoarse voice
And they attack her with a crazy fury.
Like breaking the leash of the dreaming gaze
That would like to keep them much closer to the sea.

Is wondering miss Tanta, granny is wondering
What are the seagulls from the sea doing here with us?
Look! Seagulls in the neighborhood, in the fields!
Or sky's stray dogs could they be?

Maybe they got tired of the infinity of the sea
And of her salted guids
Or maybe they would wanted to see
From where the people coming when vacationing at the sea.

Or maybe a love story they could be following
To find out what got started on the sunny beach,
Whatever the name would that be?

Entering through the horizon's door The Evening—
A good neighbor of ours
Stepping on the Sun's yard, a freshly cut blue grass
And the seagulls screaming to the hoarse voice
Pushing her with long beaks
Cutting her in a sharp flight
Thin slices to satisfy a brand new hunger...

—Our sky needed some dogs!
A startled voice says on a bench, next to us!
To bark to the dawn and to the sunset
Cause sometimes we forget about time and we too
Run away from summer!...

MASS-MEDIA STILL HATES THE POETRY TODAY

MASS-MEDIA STILL HATES THE POETRY TODAY
AND I WRITE WITH AN OAK-TREE IN A FOG...

I REMEMBER TODAY AS WELL OF THE PAST
AND THE ETER IS LIKE A BRIDGE.
TOWARDS WHICH MY LOOK SLOWLY CLIMBS
TO SEARCH FOR GENTLE OR FIERY EYES FROM WHERE
THEY COME FROM
TO SEARCH FOR OLD STORIES OF SMILE OR OF TEARS...
AND
I'M SEARCHING FOR A BENCH FOR MY TIRED GAZE
OF SO MUCH RUNNING THROUGH MEMORIES SUNSET...
AND
I'M SEARCHING FOR A WINTER FOR OUR SECRET
SNOWFALLS
SEARCHING FOR A BOAT FOR A VIOLIN
AND
I'M SEARCHING FOR A YOUTH FOR CRAZY US
AND
SEARCHING FOR A SEAGULL FOR A NEW SKY
AND
I'M SEARCHING FOR HARBORS FOR OTHER SHIPS WITH
SILKS AND VELVETS
AND
SEARCHING FOR GUIDS FOR THE UNSALTED SEAS OF THE
RAIN
MASS-MEDIA STILL HATES THE POETRY TODAY
AND I WRITE WITH AN OAK-TREE IN A FOG
A LOVE CAROL
AND THE WHIPS DON'T CRACK
THE FINGERS CRACK ON PIANOS...

TERRIBLE, NECESSARY AND ETERNAL PERVERSION

And you climbed in the cup of my palms
Up on the stairs of the marble looks
With the foggy day that scrutinized us...

And you climbed in the cup of my palms
With your body shape that was making dogs out of my eyes
Mad dogs
Bitting with dispair and with hunger
Impossible to keep them in the leash of the NO!

And you climbed in the cup of my palms
To celebrate imortality with a kiss
The kiss- the attic of the soul
With a tactile window towards infinity...

And you climbed in the cup of my palms
With your tight and soft dress
With your breasts carressing the carress...
With your lips like every moment coming out of the sea

And I was looking under your dress
When you were slowly climbing
In the cup of my palms...

EVENING WAS YOUR DRESS

Words waiting for a long time for our story
Or at least it seemed to me
In the evening
The same
As your dress...

Hooray!
The words waiting at the corner of the
interjection!
Hooray!
Same words, that were dating the meanings, as
always...
Now standing in line after "bench" and "willow"
and "dream"

I was laying my head on the stone of your
shoulder
Lying to myself that I was making a halt on my
way to infinity...
And the stone of my head was rolling hard

Was rolling over the winter holidays of my love
And was bumping to the "nowhere" and to the
"always"
To the stone of air of the clouds
Discarded towards the temple
From where rains spring...

Words waiting for a long time for our story
And they were standing in line after "a hand
shake", after "confusing", after "timid"...
Standing in line to get new meanings...
It would have been, as always,
A small apocalypse the sunset,
If it wasn't

THE SAME
AS YOUR DRESS
STRETCHED ON THE INFINITY
BECAUSE YOU WERE INFINITELY BEAUTIFUL
AND INFINITELY I WAS LOVING YOU...
AND THE KISS WOULD HAVE BEEN, MAYBE, THE LAST
STORM OF OUR WORLD

IF YOU HEAR CRACKLING, DEAR READER,
FOR SURE THERE ARE NOT THE BROKEN FRAMES OF THE
GAZE FROM THAT TIME
THAT ARE BURNING IN THE FIRE OF THE SIX
OF A DICE THROWN MAYBE TOO EARLY...

WINE

I BEG YOU! I WOULD BE MORE SERENE
IF FROM THE FIRST SNOWFALL WE WOULD MAKE DRY WINE!
LET'S ALLOW IT TO FERMENT
WHILE WE'RE RUNNING A MILE THROUGHOUT THE WORLD
A MILE OF SAD AND OF BAD AND OF LONELY...
A MILE OF PEOPLE THAT CAN'T UNDERSTAND...

I BEG YOU! I WOULD BE MORE SERENE
IF FROM THE FIRST SNOWFALL WE WOULD MAKE DRY WINE
AND WE WOULD TAKE THE WHOLE TWILIGHT
AND THE NIGHT BREEZED BY THREE FANS
PRINTED WITH RIVERS OF SNOW FLAKES
TO THE BORDER OF THE FAIRYTALES

AND THEN, LET'S DRINK DRY WINE OF SNOWFALL
FROM GLASSES
OR FROM THE BIG PLOW
OR, BETTER, FROM A FULL BALERINA!
TO COLLIDE CRYSTAL LOOKS
TO CARESS THE NIGHT'S SKIN- THE PARCHMENT OF SECRET LOVES!

TO SKIN THE SKIN OF EMPTY KISS
IN THE VOID FALLEN FROM THE SOUL'S 10TH FLOOR!
THIS WORK WILL PUT MORE SKIN ON US
MORE PEAKS
IN INTERCONNECTIVITY WHICH I WOULDN'T KNOW WHAT TO DO WITH
IN THIS POEM.

VIOLET,
TODAY BE JUST VIOLET!

Violet, today be just violet, in bloom, or evening with fairies,
Mixed breed and stretched on my thoughts and my caresses!
Be at the window overlooking the sea pored into a horizon...
You, the one that always runs away from another embrace...

Sharpen my gaze with the blades of your eyelashes
Or round it for me with hips and tighs and breasts and waist and spine
Detached maybe
From a movement
Of sea waves...?

Suddenly coming towards you, the gaze becomes snowfall
Shy bedding over your body forms
A jump from one heaven to another
Over a wall that lacks the heights...

Violet, today be just violet!
And I promise you: I'll save you from the twilight like I would from a dragon
And I'll squeeze you
In an embrace of light with gold

Let's cheer rove, at the violets New Year's eve,
Under a sun fleeing from pink color
Ignat of flowers- the frost
Is coming and we won't see them anymore...

Brake down my flower, but don't brake my color!
Eye's erruption, dear.
The dust of nothingness, stubborn.
The voice of the sheets
Clenched in a fist by the printer

Brake down my sunset, but leave me the color!
Leave me the writing of the distance
Always indecipherable
Like Gelu's longing...

AN ANTIQUE AFTERNOON

-PAINTER, WHAT DO YOU PAINT
-I PAINT MEMORIES...
NICHITA RAN AWAY FROM HOME A WEEK AGO
-CAPTAIN, I BROUGHT A PAINTER
THERE WAS A GUITAR TOO
-LET'S HEAR FROM THE PAINTER
...ALL THOSE YOUNG GIRLS
WERE LOOKING AT ME STRANGELY
I WAS UGLY, NOT HANDSOME, LIKE NICHITA...
BUT THEY WERE LISTENING WITH PLEASURE
MOTIONLESS, LEANING ON A TEMPLE
ONE ON ANOTHER'S SHOULDER
BONDED
LIKE THE HONEY WAS FLOWING FROM THEIR EARS
HONEY POURED FROM THE ABUNDANCE OF THE GUITAR'S
CHORDS...
-LET'S GO
-LET'S GO
-PAINTER, WHAT DO YOU PAINT
-MEMORIES...
I TOOK A TAXI
I DROPPED SMĂRĂNDIȚA TO HER FLAT
-LOOK, MY LOVE
I BROUGHT A PAINTER THAT RECITE FROM LABIȘ
-NICHITA, PLEASE
LEAD THE GENTLEMAN TO THE DOOR, MAYBE HE IS BUSY
-THIS PAINTER IS WONDERFUL
HE RECITES FROM LABIȘ
-YOU BROUGHT MEN LIKE THESE BEFORE NICHITA
AND THE SILVERWARE FROM MY MOTHER DISSAPEARED
...NICHITA NO
LET'S SLEEP THERE
ON THE FLOOR

ON MY BOOTS
I LEFT ON ONE FOOT TO NOT TAKE OFF NICHITA'S BOOT
FROM UNDER HIS HEAD
THE THIRD DAY
AT MY WORKSHOP COMES NICHITA
–PRINTER, WHAT DO YOU PRINT?

AUTOPORTRET WITH WINTER

And, if it would snow, would you come to the window
To look for me with your gaze from behind the naked trees
From behind silenced buildings
And from behind passers-by shoulders cleaving their teeth?

And, if it would snow, would you get up on the toes of stollen kisses
And returned wrinkled and stripped of great memories,
To look for me with your gaze on a ski slope
Invaded and forever conquered
By the horde of the more than a thousand kids?

And, if it would snow, would you get up to boil some wine
With cinnamon, so you can receive me
Warm dressed, shivering and hidden in the big white shawl?

And if it would snow

WINDOW

Look at the face of the snowfall! Is fascinating...
Did you know that the most muscles are on the face?
Look at the face of the snowfall! It's got exotic traits...
Doesn't seem to you that it's smiling?
Look at the face of the snowfall!
Still has sugar on its lips?
Or to my happiness it seems like?
Look at the face of the snowfall!
Gymnastics opportunity for the gaze
With extensions towards childhood...
One, two, three, it snows!
One, two, three, it snows!
One, two, three, it snows!
And at the left..
One, two, three, it snows!
And at the right...
One...
Two...
Three...
Slow descend downhill...
Take the snowfall to the ground,
With a straight face,
Then, slowly lift up a snowball
And higher: bloom up an iris
And higher: perfume the attic of the evening
Look at the face of the snowfall
With the wrinkles of the buildings under her beautiful eyes
Powder with beautiful neighbors, please
Powder, powder!
And
One, two, three, it snows...

THE WINE OF THAT RAIN, OLD, TOO LATE...

How good is for drinking, now
The wine of that rain, old...
But too late
To gargle to party
Champagne of wine...

The winter is yet to come
And all the rains will be frozen
Like our hands
Empty of other and cracked...

"Snows" we'll call them
And they will startle at our call
With a fairytale at each window
Broken or unbroken by a majestic bird's beak...

We will move in the zodiacs of white world!
And we will change, our beginnings, dreams.
And we will change, unthinking of, our thoughts.
And then we will change, ourselves too!

I don't like the winter but just Vivaldi's,
When it snows with warm fingers
On the horizon of keyboards
Like always in construction
Like always in alteration...

"Snows" we will call them
And "snowed" I will call myself

AT ONE TIME, I LIVED NEXT TO THE MARKET PLACE

At one time, I lived next to the market place
And the sun, first, in the morning
Would come, dazzling, at my windows
Then it will go down to a market woman

At one time, I lived next to the market place
And my windows were happy
And I was always buying images
Without waiting for a change...of shadows

It seemed like a happy world,
It seemed like a wave of desires, of hunger, of thirst,
From a sea of the love arrived
From a blooming branch a breeze seemed like...

There was a time, you were passing too shopping for flowers
It was then when I liked you,
Like I had in my gaze the second heart
Bigger seemed like, more restless than the first one...

You looked like a queen, despotic rulling with her beauty
And the air was your buttler
...Evening after evening,
The dark was blushing your absence...

When the summer was boiling,
I was adding salt of sentiment
And greens of looks in love
And aromas for olfactory wanderings...

VISION

Let's throw away our glasses!
Let's throw away our sight!
It's time, I believe, today, to find out
If even blind we would have met,
If in your hand my hand would have found
nesting...
If even without the look in love,
Snowed by the beauty, destiny would have put us
on the same bench...

It's time, I believe, today, to find out,
If we were knocking like two crystal glasses,
With shaken liquors,
And if we were pouring us,
From the same liquid spheres
On the same table, from the same chance of
destiny...

It's time, I believe, today, to find out...

And, all of sudden, lenses throw themselves in a
sea of their own
And, all of a sudden, they bump
Blind buck of twilight
And young very drunk

It's time, I believe, today, to find out
And, all of a sudden, we throw away the looks, all,
couples-couples,
And evenings with strabismus, uncoupled,
Like your dream-just one...
Like summer, gone, forgotten...

It's time, I believe, today, to find out...

IT SNOWS ON NOTHING

Carriages pulled by time
How many times
It snows on nothing
And the layer of love
Grows always like a dough...

Carriages pulled by time
How many times
Horses give checkmate to distances
And they always grow too
Like a dough...

Carriages pulled by time
How many times
I fall and I roll
To the sea
And arrive next to your ankles...

SO WHAT?

You were born dazzling
Of beer foam and of sea
From diaphanous kisses
Between Dia and Phanous
And you grew up under a busy sky of seagulls
Like a blue tram lost up somewhere…
Still waiting at the windows facing the sea
Dreams- beautiful crazy dreams
Blondes, redhair or brunes,
Made you each morning even more beautiful
And your first kiss was of a wind
Of waves
And of shores
And of though…
And, when to get married
With one of the thousand rich ones
I stole you with a "wouldn't be beautiful if…"
Crying out loud that I am sick of sea and custom!
That I hear the seagulls calling me: „daddyyy"
And you: „mommyyyy"!
And the waves from my voice you were listening
When I was speaking to you…
~what a liquid choir…

MY SEA WAS CALLED: THE UNITED STATES OF THE BEAUTIFUL RAINS OF SUMMER

OR THE WINE THAT DROWNED ME
THE NIGHT BEFORE
I LOCKED YOU IN OPEN ARMS!
I GAVE YOU A SET OF WATERCOLORS OF ROSES...
TO PAINT ME ANYWAY YOU WANT!
TO DOODLE ANY BAD THOUGHT THAT COULD BE WRITTEN...

PINK IOANA

WE'RE TALKING, LOVING...AND MAYBE EVEN WE...
LITURGY, FASTING, BLESSING AND MAYBE EVEN WE...
SPUN IN THE STRING OF MIRUNA...
THE SPINNING OF THAT EVENING...
SPININGS AND RETURNS...

FREED FROM THE WOOL OF THE DAWN
I ADOR TO TOUCH THE SILK OF YOUR WORDS
ALL THE WAY TO THE SEA
TO TOUCH IT
ALL THE WAY TO YOUR SLIM ANKLES

WHEN YOU INTRODUCED YOURSELF THE MORNING WAS
PINK
ON THE SEASHORE
AND YOU DIN'T WEAR ANOTHER SHIRT BUT THAT LIGHT

WHEN YOU TOOK THAT SHIRT OFF
I FORGOT YOU...
IN THE MEANING OF THE SUNRAYS...

TODAY, WE JUST TALK...
SILKY WORDS BY THE METER
OR TO INFINITY...

NO!
ARE NOT VERY USEFUL TODAY THE MOST BEAUTIFUL
MEMORIES!
I AM AFRAID THEY'LL GET BLUNT...

THE WOMAN PLAYING PIANO ON ME

Like she was descending on the snowfalls stairs...
Her simple existence was kissing the world
And it would make her smile
Or blush...
She, browned in the silk oven,
She, bloomed
From never seen white buds of snowfalls.
She was playing piano on me
Calling my name...

What can I give
For her to call me again,
With the name of the light of this day?
Pink light like a skating rink
On which I fall
In the sunsets with all four seasons of the
colors
Ah! How beautiful the seasons of the color BLUE!

Like she was descending on the snowfalls stairs...
Her touches were the Sunday of my skin!
Were a wind tuning violins

Not touching the fields grass of my childhood
When un-hearing the bells rang for later
Bone of the attacker in the breathed plains...

MAY 13TH AT THE BEACH

THIS POEM DOESN'T START WITH A CAPITAL LETTER, BUT WITH LETTER OF THE SEA!
...WITH LETTERS OF THE SEA!
WITH LETTERS WITH WHICH WE ARE CALLING HER
THE ONE TO WHERE WE ARE GOING TO UNINVITED BUT ONLY BY THE DESTINY
AND WHEN WE NEED LIQUIDITY:
FEELINGS, ILUSIONS, DREAMS AND OTHER- TONS- TONS OF HUMANITY...

AT THE BEACH! NAME OF THE SOUL'S PAWNSHOP AND OF BANK OF HUMANITY!
TO HER WE PAWN AND MORTGAGE GREAT LOVES, IDEA OF LIBERTY
THE PARTYING FEELING...

EVERYTHING STARTS FROM HERE! ALL SOUL ROADS TAKE US HERE: AT THE BEACH!

FROM THE SEA WAVES YOU'VE TAKEN FLIGHT, YOU, MAJESTIC BIRD.
FROM THE SEA WAVES YOU'VE WALKED, YOU, WOMAN CRAZY BEAUTIFUL.
FROM THE SEA WAVES YOU'VE TAKEN YOUR RUN, SILLY CHILD.
FROM THE SEA WAVES YOU'VE TAKEN YOUR RAIN, RAIN!
ALL THE WORLD'S BIRDS FLYING WITH THE FLIGHT TAKEN FROM WAVES OF THE SEA
ALL THE WOMEN OF THE WORLD WALKING WITH THE WALK TAKEN FROM WAVES OF THE SEA.
ALL THE KIDS OF THE WORLD RUNNING WITH A BROKEN RUN FROM THE WAVES OF THE SEA
ALL THE RAINS RAINING WITH DROPS TAKEN FROM WAVES OF THE SEA...

ALL THE FLOWERS OF THE WORLD BLOOMING FROM
GRAINS OF FORM OF THE WAVES OF THE SEA

I CAME, SEA, TO YOU.
TO WATCH YOUR FOAMY WAVES
AND TO LET THEM TO CLIMB INTO MY EYES
FUTURE TEARS
WITH WHICH I CAN CRY MY JOY AND ALL SADNESS...

FROM THE WAVES OF THE SEA ROLLED DOWN UNSEEN
DICE
AND THE SAND HID THEM ALL OF A SUDDEN
WITHOUR SEEING WHAT THEY ROLLED, AT LEAST ONCE,
WITHOUT SEEING OUR DESTINY IN THE FACE!

I DON'T KNOW SINCE WHEN I STAYED AT THE SEA
BUT
YOU ARE COMING TOWARDS ME, FROM THE WORD
"HAPPINESS",
AND I AM:
IN LOVE, CONTRASTING, UNFULFILLED...

...I DON'T KNOW WHY I AM STILL AT THE BEACH TODAY
LIKE ALWAYS,
LIKE AGAIN SPECIAL GARNISHES
OF DREAM AND OF FLOWER
GO AND GO AWAY TOWARD THE SEA'S DISTANCE
AND THEY TAKE ME AND TAKE ME AND TAKE ME...
WITH THE WHOLE ECHO, WITH ECHO WITH ECHO

LET'S DESCEND AGAIN THE TRAIL OF THE MOUNTAIN TO
THE SHORE
HIM LIMESTONE,
WE EMPTY STEP, ERRODED BY CURIOSITY,
TO DESCEND WITH THE BEACH TOWEL IN THE BAG IT'S
BEACH DAY
TODAY IS NUDISM DAY! IS MONDAY
WHEN SERIOUS PEOPLE GO TO WORK
AND THE ONES WITH UNSPEAKEABLE DEEDS IN MIND

TAKE A DAY OFF
FROM WHATEVER DAYS THEY HAVE LEFT
FROM PERMITTED FREE DAYS
THROUGH LAWS AND THROUGH DREAMS!
DON'T BE TOO SHY! WHY TO BUILDING OBSTACLES
OURSELVES?
BE JUST A LITTLE...
JUST TILL WHEN YOU TAKE OFF
WHATEVER YOU WEAR UNDER YOUR JEANS...
I DON'T KNOW HOW WOULD AN INVITATION SOUND LIKE
FOR THE UNDRESSING EVENT...
NAKED, NAKED, NAKED, NAKED...
WHAT IS STILL FULL?
ONLY THE WINE GLASS!

POEM IN THREE TIMELINES

I

Let's talk about the language of summers at the beach!
Or about the arrivals at the beach...
Let's talk about the language of the sunsets
One on top of the other to set
One from the other to rise
Like some suns
Like some titans
Like some idols...
Let's talk about the language of the light
The official one
In mornings- endless countries
Let's talk about the heat of the stoves with the snowfall view...
Let it snow from our words
Over tympanum-body.
Over awaiting- body...
Or let's get outside pur and simple silent
And the door of each room
And each window
Be covers of a fairytale
Every unspoken word-cover of sentiment. of feeling...
Let's kiss just for the sake of the kiss

Let's write the date of once upon a time
In the notebooks and to throw them away
To fly with the thought like a thought

FROM THE LIED TO MINDS OF EX STUDENTS
TEMPORAL FAILING STUDENTS...

LET'S ALL WEAR READING GLASSES...OF MIRACLES
US TO RAIN THE SKY TOO
TODAY
TO SNOW IT
WHY WOULD'T US BE PERSEIDS?

II

IN THE EVENINGS LOST IN SHADES.
I AM AN ANGELSCRAPER
IN A METROPOLIS OF FEELINGS
WHERE THE HOBOS ARE ONLY THE BAD PEOPLE!

IN THE EVENINGS LOST IN SHADES.
I AM WRITING FOR THE OLD TEMPERANCES TO PULL
SHIPS SUNKEN IN RAINS
AND TO STRETCH AGAIN THEIR SAILS
FROM THE STEP TO THE KISS AND CARESS
FROM THE SMILE TO THE RUN
FROM THE WRITING TO THE DREAM
FROM THE LOVE TO THE LAUGH

IN THE EVENINGS LOST IN SHADES
SEA: LIKE AN ELONGATED RAIN
ASLEEP

III

I WOULD PREFER TO NOT ASK ME HOW AM I DOING!
LIKE NO ONE ASKS THE SUN HOW IS DOING
KNOWING THAT HE RISES, SHINES.

Gives life
And goes down!
It's a state:
Is the spring of the seas:
Blinding blooming-liquid petals
Endless blooming. In purple evenings
A waving lilac with perfume of distances
Waterfalls of shadows of blooming magnolias
Stretched waves like some arms
I am in a hurry to step barefoot on the buds of the sand
What will never break in hourglasses.
On large beaches
Long to lay myself
How long my soul lasts...
For how long my soul will last...

GODESS – ARCHIPELAGO OF FLESH AND DREAM

It was time to introduce myself to the horizon!

I was floating to return
To my Itaca
On a sea like a huge winespritz
Compasses– migratory birds
Sails canvases painted by evening rains ...
Air currents breathed by the gods
And the birds
Drunk on imensity...
They seemed to know me

Lead me to the sunset,
If other way you don't know
At the archipelago of flesh
I will stop
In algae of embraces
Braided with evenings and with rains

And it was time to introduce myself to the horizon...

IF ONE DAY YOU'D BE MY SHEET OF PAPER

DREAMING: HOW BEAUTIFUL IT WOULD BE
IF ONE DAY
OR AN EVENING
YOU WOULD BE MY SHEET OF PAPER
I COULDN'T ERASE IT OR RIP IT
IT WOULD BE AN ETERNAL WRITING, UNREPEATABLE,
IMPOSSIBLE TO CHANGE AND TO CORRECT A FATAL POEM!
SO THAT'S WHY
I DREAM TO WRITE ON YOUR NAKED BODY
A FATAL POEM
UNIQUE
UNREPEATABLE...
AND YOU WOULD LAY ON THE BED LIKE A SHEET OF
PAPER
AND I WILL WATCH VOLUPTUOUSLY AS ALWAYS
YOUR UNWRITTEN WHITE, INDESCRIBABLE...LIKE SNOWED...
OF AN ENDLESS BEAUTY...
AND I WOULD START MAYBE FROM THE SHOULDERS, FROM
THE NECK WITH THE FIRST WORD
WHICH WOULD BE ...KISS...
AND I WOULD WRITE
I WOULD FATALLY WRITE
AND NO! I WOULDN'T PUT THE FINAL PERIOD...
I WOULD LEAVE LIKE THAT NEXT TO THE ANKLES
ONE WORD: ALWAYS...
AND THEN I WOULD ASK YOU TO MAKE A FEW STEPS
BECAUSE I ALWAYS LIFT UP THE PAPER AND I READ IT
AND I ADMIRE IT WRITTEN
AND I SMELL IT LIKE AN INK FLOWER
-YES! THE INK BLOOMS IN POEMS, YOU KNOW!-
AND YOU WALKING ON WRITTEN: WHAT A POEM
THE POEM OF MY POEM'S ABOUT A POEM

WHICH I WOULD WRITE
IF THE POEM OF YOUR WONDER
WOULD LIT ME UP WITH A LIGHTNING OF A BEAUTIFUL
MADNESS

WHEN LOVE MEETS WORDS...

I PUSHED YOUR HAIR ASIDE A BIT
AND I HUNG ON YOUR EAR
AN AUDITORY EARRING:
A WHISPER OF LOVE...
A BREEZE BORROWED BY ME FROM THE BărăGAN PLAIN
SOMETIME AGO, WHEN I WAS A CHILD
AND I WAS LISTENING LIFE AND I SAW IT WITH MY
MAXIMUM DREAMING...
NO. YOU WERE NOT EXPECTING IT
BUT IT SEEMED THAT YOU WERE WAITING THAT EVERY
SHIP BROUGHT BY THE WAVE OFFSHORE...GUIDE OF
OFFSHORE...
LIKE ANY SAILS LIFTED THE BREEZE THAT PUSHES
TOWARDS THE UNSEEN WONDERS...
IT WAS ME THIS TIME
COMING FROM NOWHERE AND NEVER
I KNOW. AND YOU KNOW.
I WILL LEAVE. ONE DAY. IN AN INSTANT...
YOU WILL LOSE THE NECKLACES OF KISSES FROM YOUR
NECK
YOU WILL LOSE THE AUDITORY EARRINGS OF MY
WHISPERS
YOU WILL LOSE THE TACTILE BRACELET OF HOLDING
HANDS
YOU WILL LOSE THE LIPSTICK OF STOLEN KISSES FROM
YOUR LIPS BY ME
TO GIFT THEM TO YOUR SOUL
YOU WILL LOSE THE WONDERFUL PULSATION WHEN THE
UNIVERSE'S CLOCK SEEMED TO BE US
YOU WILL LOSE THEM NOT OUT OF YOUR INATTENTION
OR MINE...

YOU WILL LOSE THEM OUT OF INATTENTION OF OUR
DESTINY
OF LOSERS...
AND IF IT WERE TO LOSE, LET'S GET LOST!
...BUT UNTIL THEN, WE WILL WASTE TIME
BEAUTIFULLY...

SILVER STOVE

Is keeping me warm, in the night
Like a cloud expansion.
A silver stove
Inside which the moon burns

The night opened her mouth
To bite into the world
Is chewing us with teeth of whispers
Crunchy of pesimists
Shaken of black spasms
In an August without direction.

JUST BE!

BE LIKE A SLAMMED DOOR!
LIKE A SUN SMASHED ON WINDOWS
LIKE A RAIN HITTING THE WINDOW SILLS
LIKE A MOON BUMPING INTO VENUS STAR
BE THAT'S ALL!

BEYOND THE QUESTIONS
EARLIER THAN ANSWERS
ALWAYS FURTHER
IN THE RUSH OF THE HORSES TOWARDS THEIR SEAS

BE, BUT JUST BE FOR GOODNESS SAKE!

EVENING-FRAME AND BRAZILIAN SARA

There are people
That like to live their
Life like an exhibition
Of the eyes
Sipping coffee
Swinging the left leg over the right leg
And then it has to be peace.
It has to be end of day and of problems...
And then,
They have to watch you in the evening-frame
Startled by their painter's dream
In its pink period
Spledour in movement
In running
In kissing
In love
In sea
In the spectaculous movement of their longing

But you can't be painted
You
Coming and going every second
Like a dream
Impatient to be concrete
Tu
Are Beautiful
Nobel Prize for erotism!
Brazilian Sara
You tame racists
You men-gastropods
To step on
Going toward ideals

IF I HAVEN'T MET YOU IN THE MINIBUS OF
PLOIESTI-BALACA...

THE ELEGY OF THE STARS

This poem is not written in the cable car!
Neither on the mall's escalator!
I am tired of climbing invisible stair steps
But I climb and I'm still climbing...
And I believe I will be
In a later part of life,
Like a child of Universe,
In the attic of the snowfalls...
And of torential rains
Older than our tears...
And I climb and I'm still climbing...
And I don't know what I am searching for anymore
On the peaks of the mountain, in the future like
an attic of an old house...
I climb. That's all.

I am tired to keep climbing.
I am tired of " that's all ".

I don't know anymore what I am searching for...
I climb: what of hunger for steps, for stairs,
Of "climbing", to have an Olympus
To see how miracles bloom and greenish the world,
And how the horizon could transform itself in
miracles
How they flow in the cups of the eyes like
visual champagnes...
I would love to believe that I climb towards
summer
And I will stop only when I'm thirsty of the wine
drunk with you.

GARGLED AND PASSED THROUGH LION'S TEETH STUCK ON
THE NECK OF A LIONESS
AND MESSED UP IN THE HEAD AND SOUL.
I WANT TO RINSE MY BEING
WITH YOUR CLEAR TEAR!
I WANT TO GET DRUNK MY THOUGHTS
WITH YOU!
TO CLIMB TOGETHER ON THE CARRIAGE STEPS
AND, ON THE WAY,
TO SHATTER THE HORIZON WASHED BY RAIN
OF AN EVENING, LIKE A DIURNAL APOSTROPHE
OR LIKE AN EXCLAMATION POINT
OR QUESTION MARK...
OF DIURNAL ENUNCIATION...

WINTER PAINTING WITH FIRE IN THE STOVE

Sometimes, when I lay down
Is like boundlessness wacked me...
Other times, when I want to relax
From too much sitting in the office,
I have the impression that
My bones crackle like the wood inside the stove,
Even between fairytales spaces,
Next to yellow lights on the white wall,
Like some petals,
That will make you believe, looking at them,
That even the fire can bloom:
The rose given to the eyes that knows
To paint the world differently...

In what fire do I burn?
And what makes me so jittery?
Love- gasoline put on fire!
Sweet whispers- breeze that intensifies me
My bones crackle like wood in the fire...

I feel like painted in a winter painting with fire
in the stove
And I feel the need to lay down
Until my utopia crackles.
The stories flow, the time stops,
I am soaking the present in the evening ink bottle
And everything is meaningless written
In the sky
How clearly we read from earth
Our destiny
So far away written...
Like we know it...

HOW SIMPLE I GET ON MY KNEES, MOTHER,
AND KISS THE EARTH
AND I KNOW AND I READ
I AM MELTING MYSELF
HOW EASY I SEE EVERYTHING ONE MORE TIME
HOW MUCH I WILL MISS IT
WHAT A WINTER! HOW COLD!
I FEEL MY BONES CRACKLING LIKE WOOD INSIDE THE STOVE
TO WARM UP AGAIN AN INSTANT OF LOVE.

CONFESSION

I GOT LOST BETWEEN WORDS
TRYING TO GET TO YOUR NAME.
ASKING MYSELF IF I CAN CALL YOU
WITHOUT MURKYING THE SILENCE OF THE WONDERS
WITHOUT MURKYING THE BLOOMING OF OTHER SOULS
THEM, IN LOVE WITH YOU TOO
TO WHICH YOU ARE FIRST AND LAST SUMMER...
AND I CALLED YOU IN A THOUGHT
GETTING ON MY KNEES LIKE A CHILD

IN FACT...

In fact, the rain never stops!
In fact, there aren't more rains!
There is a single rain with her pauses, with her replays,
With her rhythm changes
And setting...and her rainbows...
It will be stupid to believe it will stop...
Rain and love never stop...

REMEMBER IN THREE TIMELINES

I sit again today
On the small chair
Of wooden linden flowers -
The only thing that I have left
From my childhood heaven's box.
I am sitting at the window with autumn
Like a shore of rains.
Lost in an eclipse
Too long
Too sad...

Watching the fire of dry leaves
Too rushed
Too red
Too high
I watch the fire of dry leaves
Like of a star with an edge stuck in the ground.
Longing for the sky
With a thousands of edges reaching burning
towards it.
Succeeding only to enter into an earthy sextile
with a petunia...

I swore to never offer you a diamond!
Because you wore on all wrists
The absolute beauty and shine!
Every step of yours
Made ten white doves fly
And your evening dress with snowfall
Waving the gaze like a sea of a soul...
Each gesture of yours made 100 butterflies fly.
Each gaze of yours blooming me up like a garden.

Today I don't hitchhike anymore.
Maybe that's why I don't get to you.
Today I don't have that many dreams anymore
Maybe that's why the night is much longer
Than the branches of the secular willows...
Too long to get to a morning
Where to drink my coffee with you.
Mask

Just arrived to the carnival.
Was raining
I chose a black cloak
And a Nordic mask
Maybe Celtic.
Maybe Visighotic...
You were dressed like the priestess of Apollo's temple.
And !..with my hideous mask...
I approached you like a barbarian
You got scared so bad when you saw me
That
You screamed loudddddly
Your loud scream
Was longer than a long train
And passed much faster than the fastest train
Through all the train stations of my soul
Without stopping
At any of them...
Your long scream
Put with its power the mask on my face
So well
That I was afraid that it will stick to my skin
And I could never get rid of it...

Just arrived to the carnival.
Was raining
I chose a black cloak
And a Nordic mask
Maybe Celtic.

MAYBE VISIGHOTIC...
YOU WERE DRESSED LIKE THE PRIESTESS OF APOLLO'S TEMPLE.
AND I..WITH MY HIDEOUS MASK...
I APPROACHED YOU LIKE A BARBARIAN
YOU GOT SCARED SO BAD WHEN YOU SAW ME
AND YOU RAN AWAY WITH A SCARAB- WHAT AN IMBECILE COSTUME

LOST IN A GERBERA TRIANGLE

At that time I was alone...
At that time I had just one eyelid...
Closing my eyes with the sea
Or with the distance,
Which were useful, one at a time,
By the virtue of the blessed universal harmony,
Like the second eyelid.
And, this way, I got to dream
To rest.
To retire inside myself unseen
And to descend into my soul dear things
On stairsteps of silence and thought...
At that time I was alone...
Lost in a gerbera triangle
In a geometry
Unknown
And it was raining with rains of dew on
Boulevards of color
Sprinkled with red
And yellow and white
And
Buildings of perfume
And neighborhoods of petals
And I am searching like crazy
Awaken from a dream
The dew shadows
Taste, sight, smell, hearing...a wall, a window
The sun
A thought, another thought then other-woolf
packs- I am awake.
I touch
I feel the wine wrinkles

I FEEL THE WRINKLES OF YOUR DRESS
THEY ARE THOUGHTS THAT WRINKLE
THE TRANSLUCID SHINE, STILL, OF THE DRY WINE.
POUR ME CHAMPAGNE
IN SOUL
I AM THE CRAZIEST GLASS
THAT CANNOT STAND ON ONE LEG ANYMORE
DENTIST OF MY WISDOM TEETH.
THE WINE.
OR MAYBE RAIN OR SEA, OR MAYBE
INFINITY'S KISS
OR KITE TOO HIGH FLOWN
TAKEN
BY THE STRONG CURRENTS.
AND TAKEN INTO A DIFFERENT SKY
WHERE OTHER RAINS GET BORED
AND OTHER SNOWFALLS WAIT FOR TIME TRAINS...
I AM ADAM WITH HALF TIME
TU ARE EVE FROM NIGHT SHIFT.
AH!
WHEN IT RAINS EVERYTHING IT'S A CATHEDRAL
AND WEEP THE UNSEEN INVISIBLE SAINTS
ICONOSTASIS
SILENCE IN BURSTING LAUGHS
AND RAIN
TO DIG INTO SEAS FOUNDATIONS
FOR COLUMNS OF NEW SUNSETS
WATCHED BY LOVERS
DECIPHERED BY FREAKS
ADMIRED BY PEOPLE WITH TIME.
WHEN IT RAINS IT'S A HUGE CATHEDRAL
AND IF IT WOULD STOP WHAT WOULD CHANGE BETWEEN
DREAMS AND REALITY
WHAT A PARTING OF DREAMS
OF TEARS OF THOUGHTS...
AND ALL OF A SUDDEN
A HAPPENING LIFTED FROM ARMPITS!
A BURST OF LAUGH
REACTIONARY

YES...IT AMUSES ME HOW SERIOUS WE ARE
HOW TENSE
HOW WE LOVE TO DEATH
HOW WE ARE RIGHT
HOW WE WIN AND LOSE.
HOW WE TRIUMPH AND MISS!IT AMUSES ME HOW YOU
HATE ME
HOW YOU ENVY ME
AND HOW YOU STRUGGLE TO HURT ME
THE BARKING AMUSES ME
THE GROWLING AMUSES ME
AND WITH LAUGHING LIKE THAT MY LIFE PASSES BY.
WHAT COULD THIS BE?
A BREATH...
A BREATH ON WHICH I WALK LIKE ON A STRING
AND HOW MUCH I WON'T WANT TO
GET UNBALANCED AND TO FALL
...IN HISTORY.

DNA OF THE SEAS

Look at the waves on the shore
Like running
Like playing
Like some children playing outside
More and more curious
Aproaching closer and closer
To our beach towels.
To the ankles
What an endearring embrace
Maybe the sea to bring back the kid I was?
Today I am longing for myself
Look at the waves on the shore
Like running
Like playing
Like some children playing outside
More and more curious
Aproaching closer and closer
To our beach towels.
What a warm embrace
Like a stove of the soul
Look at the waves on the shore
Like running
Like playing
Like they are some children playing outside
More and more curious
Aproaching closer and closer
To our beach towels.
Like some liquid deer
Some curious children!
Like are searching rubies in us
With their smiles
From sun

RIPPED OFF LIKE SOME IMPERFECT SHEETS OF PAPER
OF DESTINY
AND THROWN IN THE MEMORY
...SEA WHERE WE WILL ALWAYS RETURN!
LOOK AT THE WAVES ON THE SHORE
LIKE RUNNING
LIKE PLAYING
LIKE THEY ARE SOME CHILDREN PLAYING OUTSIDE
MORE AND MORE CURIOUS
APROACHING CLOSER AND CLOSER
TO OUR BEACH TOWELS.
THEY FOUND LAPIS LAZULI
AND THEY MADE A SLIDE
OVER THE STONE-MIRROR- OF SUNSET
THEY WILL STEAL OUR SLIPPERS
IF WE WON'T PAY ATTENTION
AND THEY WILL TAKE THEM TO THE SEA
LIKE A GAME
THEY WILL STEAL THE RINGS AND THE BRACELETS AND
THE WALLETS
IF WE WON'T PAY ATTENTION
AND THEY WILL TAKE THEM TO THE SEA
LIKE A GAME
THEY WILL STEAL OUR NOTEBOOKS
IF WE WON'T PAY ATTENTION
AND THEY WILL TAKE THEM TO THE SEA
IN A PROVIDENTIAL GAME
...TO STOP COMPLAINING OF LACK OF TIME
OF TOO MANY THINGS TO DO...
RIGHT...I BELIEVE THAT I STILL HAVE THE DNA OF THE
SEAS

SHUT UP!

No, it wasn't me speaking!
I was sculpting the air
When the air seemed to me like it was an imens word
Spoken by gods...
No, it wasn't me speaking!
I was sculpting the air
With an echo chisel
Lost in me
To get to it
To the word spoken by gods
To discover it
Beyond the sunset
 - Sculpting the evening, because it was quieter
To not blunt my soul and mind chisel of noises
And of birds
And of sighs
And of smiles-
No it wasn't me speaking
I was silently sharp as a chisel
Stuck in the granite body of the sunset
Still looking for the concrete form of their words
Of gods from where I was born
Holding their echo in my cry and in my laugh

From the chisel blows of my soul
In the blue body of the sunset
Jumping up the silence, the too late and the music
Jumping on the sidewalks
In the night gowns of our passage on earth

This is how I lear to shut up
And to speak

Always looking the word
Spoken by the parents gods.

THE MOMENT TEMPLE

Don't ask me
Who rings the bells of silence
And neither for who!

What a pitty that on silences grass doesn't grow!

With blue fingers of evening
My gaze worships the snowfall.

Even now I see the white heart
Pulsing in a trail of a goat

Don't ask me
Who rings the bells of silence
And neither for who!

On the asphalt-thought
The lights from the gas lamp
Draw shadows for me
Colored with soul.
Nieces of chimeras
Looked at today with eyes of pepper
Of rains and snowfalls and of yourselves...

Don't ask me
Who rings the bells of silence
And neither for who!

This celebration
Burns time crackling in a longing fire
And I feel like a candle lit up inside my troat
When
The wax of last rays

FLOWS ON THE GROUND

DON'T ASK ME
WHO RINGS THE BELLS OF SILENCE
AND NEITHER FOR WHO!

OVER MY SILENCE.
YOUR BREATH SNOWS:
WHAT A LAYER IS LAYING ON MY TEMPLES. ON MY SOUL...
WHITE SHOW APPLAUDED IN MIND

REVERENCE...

CRAZY EARTH

No, is not fair to say,
That without you I'm a fool!
I will forget you like all the other ones
And, read again, will remain all just empty words!
No, is not fair to say what I feel now,
When everything ashes will become...

Is not fair to desire you up to the word
And up to the scream and ink,
Up to the barbarian bite!
Up to the kidnappings and wastages...

In the flesh of the body of a dazzling beauty
I am sticking my beast's claws
And I am tearing you apart in crazy kisses
And I am drinking you in gulps and in laughs
Lost in of the skin dunes!

I better shut up
And let the volcano's moment to errupt when I
desire you
To overflow over the valleys of your body and
thought
I better shut up
And listen to
Storm inside my chest
And I will let it throw stars on the sky in
crafted nights
And to break down all the cheap deeds
World to roll us
And dizzy to laugh or to scream like an idiot,
Venus stars to run among crazy herbs
And the horses to lead them to snails and to
runes.

TO SNATCH THE SILENCES OF THE SEAS OF THE MOON
AND TO ROLL ME THE SUNS
UNTIL MY SHADOW WITHOUT BENCHMARK WILL BE A
POOR ORPHAN
MORGANA GIRL

AND THEN, ON A ROW AND ON A VERSE,
AND ON AN OUTCRY
THE WORDS WILL STREEP OF SENSES
AND WILL THROW THEMSELVES IN QUIETENESS LIKE IN A
SEA
AND WILL MAKE FROM CUES HANGERS
AND WILL STAY SPOKEN HERE AND THERE
TOO FREE AND TOO NUDES THROUGH A WORLD
THAT DOESN'T WANT THEM ANYMORE
AND DOESN'T MISS THEM ANYMORE...
AND MAYBE WILL BE TOLD
ONLY BY SEAGULLS
JUST BY QUARTERS OR HALFS...

NO, IS NOT FAIR TO FEEL YOU THROUGH THE SILK OF
YOUR WORDS
TO FEEL YOUR WRISTS OF DESIRE CREEPING UP
AND THE FLESH OF THE DREAMS RAISED IN YOUR BREATH
I WILL FORGET YOU AND EVERYTHING WILL PASS, I
SWEAR!
AH, I MASSAGE YOU WITH A SONG ABOUT ME WITH A
SMILE ON CHAINS
FROM WHERE YOU START TO THE PEAK OF YOUR
ENDLESSNESS!

WHAT CRAZY ORCHESTRA IS, TO PLAYING TO LOVE YOU
AND VIOLINS AND LIPS
AND DRUMS AND TROAT
AND TRUMPETS AND ARMPITS
AND DOUBLE BASS AND NAPE
AND PIANO AND BUTTOCKS AND BACK
AND HARPSICHORD AND TIGHS AND
I DON'T KNOW HOW AND I DON'T KNOW WHEN ANYMORE
CRAZY EARTH!

AND WHAT A POET WAS I WHEN "IS SNOWING!" – I RANTED!

And you came to the window
Like a bird on a branch!

Looking...
Long gaze in the distance...
It looked like you had a stone in your eye
To cut with it anything in the horizon!

In the room of the secret ceremonies,
Stepping on the solemn air with barefoot long hair,
I am asking the mirrors-fields:
Would we again, be someday, children?

Poet being
When ranting
"Is snowing!"
Poem from a single word, that lights up the gaze...

We were living just autumns, in a printing of Renoir,
Dazzling evenings poured from the glass
At the same terrace where the leaves were dancing
When the cold northern winds were singing...
And winter again!
And again "Is snowing!"– I ranted
And again you came to the window...

WHAT A SONG
FROM ONE WORD...
WHAT A THOUGHT
WHAT YEARS!
WHAT AN AMALGAM...

REMEMBER IN THREE TIMELINES

I sit again today
On the small chair
Of wooden linden flowers –
The only thing that I have left
From my childhood heaven's box.
I am sitting at the window with autumn
Like a shore of rains.
Lost in an eclipse
Too long
Too sad...
Watching the fire of dry leaves
Too rushed
Too red
Too high
Watching the fire of dry leaves
Like of a star with an edge stuck in the ground.
Longing for the sky
With thousands of edges reaching burning towards it.
Succeeding only to enter into an earthy sextile with a petunia...
I swore to never offer you a diamond!
Because you wore on all wrists
The absolute beauty and shine!
Every step of yours
Made ten white doves fly
And your evening dress with snowfall
Waving the gaze like a sea of a soul...
Each gesture of yours made 100 butterflies fly.
Each gaze of yours blooming me up like a garden.
Today I don't hitchhike anymore.
Maybe that's why I don't get to you.

Today I don't have that many dreams anymore
Maybe that's why the night is much longer
Than the branches of the secular willows...
Too long to get to a morning
Where to drink my coffee with you.

FOR ELISE, WHERE ELISE IS NOT ELISE...

Why did the sea care?
And why the people from the shore of the words care?
The summer was sitting next to us
Like a voyeur
Whispering a wind
Whispering an evening
Twilighted by red
Twilighted by wine
Twilighted from a ruby...
Why did the sea care?
And why the people from the shore of the words care?
We passed the buoy of looks
On the sea, we were playing like in the attic of the rains
We kissed or we built a castle from breathings?
What are you looking at, summer?! I screamed naked
But the sea just didn't care
Unfinished like a superb story
The drawing of the day didn't fit on the sheet of my gaze
Something won't be seen
You can't put on stage pants!
What stage?! The waves bursting on the sand were liquid applauds...
Why would the sea care?
And why the people from the shore of the words care?
Adam's coast guard
Caught you at your own ease

In the drift of the desires
Mimiking a sailor that was laughing till he cried
Why would the sea care?
And why the people from the shore of the words care?
You are the wonder that painted me
From that second I remained a painting!
A painting with a happy man you named it
And you let it be erased by an evening!
What are you looking at, summer? We erased ourselves! We will erase ourselves...
From the black train station, the flowers get on an air train
To the sky, to the blue train station...
What are you looking at, summer? Everybody travels! Everybody is making love!
What a surprise for my taste buds
When they startled the coffee kissing with the sugar...
I pushed your hair aside
And I hung on your ear an auditory earring:
A love whisper...
A breeze borrowed from sea
Listening to life with the dreaming with the volume at maximum...
No. You didn't expected it
What a courage, some guts
You were a ship
The wave that is taking off shore...flux and reflux
The breeze that pushes towards unseen miracles...
It was me this time
Showing up from nowhere and from never
What are you looking at, summer?
We ran away from death in a love
Elise was stronger than vodka
I was drinking every night like crazy
How could I ever stop?!

Why would the sea care?
And why the people from the shore of the words care?
Take care of your own shine summer

I know. And you know.
I will leave. Someday. In an instant…
You will lose the neckleses of kisses from your neck
You will lose the auditory earrings of my whispers
You will lose the tactile bracelet of holding hands
You will lose the lipstick of the kisses stolen from your lips
To gift them to the soul
You will lose that wonderful pulsation
When the engine of the universal clock seemed to be us
You will lose them not out of your carelesness or mine…
You will lose them out of carelessness of our destiny
Of losers…
And if it is to lose ourselves. Then let's!
…We will both waste our time beautifully…
Now. Right now.
The moon was drawn again
With the same colors
Will fall on the concrete and iron snails. Or fabric
Over the waves
Over our bodies
And only us will catch her in our arms.

I don't know who pushed me on the steps of falling in love
But I am grateful you caught me
You caught me dreaming

YOU CAUGHT ME LOVING
YOU CAUGHT ME WANTING

...AND NOW WHAT WOULD YOU DO (TO ME)?

WHY WOULD THE SEA CARE?
AND WHY THE PEOPLE FROM THE SHORE OF THE WORDS
CARE?

YOU ARE THE STONE THAT BROKE ALL MY WINDOWS
YOU ARE THE GLAZIER THAT REPLACED THEM WITH
A MOON, A SUN, AN EVENING, A SEA,
A TREE, A SHE, A HE
EVEN THE BAUDELAIRE'S ALBATROSS,
A MANGOOSE, A WHOLE, A NOTHING,
A GOBLET, A PIG...
LATELY IT WORKS WITH IT
IN THE BABEL CALLED BOOKS

TO BETTER ENTER THE HAPINESS WITHDRAWAL

To be stupid
To not care!
To not know!

The red sunset...Scarlet...
Carmen...Carmina?!
Yes! That was your name!
No! I don't want to visit the twilight

I have to go! To get back home!
I have a hamster to feed
Indifference hamster...

I know. I am too terestrial today!
At least I am not a surveyor in India!
I could have measured the Everest and maybe at a certain time
I would get high up on the spirit's peaks
Not today!
Alcohol level 0 !
I didn't drink love!
I am not drooling anymore
Spit doesn't hurt anymore!

WOMAN-ORANGE

I DO LIKE TO KNOW YOU
TO DISCOVER YOU
IS LIKE I WOULD PEEL
AND OPEN AN ORANGE FROM GREECE, SWEET
TO THE BLUE SKY
LIKE A SHARD OF A STAIN GLASS WINDOW
OF A VOIVODESHIP PALACE
TO THE DIZZYING SEA
TO THE WHITE STONES IN THE SUN
SWEET TO MY EMBRACE
TO MY KISS
TO MY DREAMS!
WHAT A BEAUTIFUL ENDLESSNESS
OF A SWEET
WOMAN-ORANGE!

RECITATIONS

The rain recites
Recites a sea
The sea recites
Recites a rain
I recite sick
From you
You recite sick
From me
We recite our loneliness and we overlap it
And it is so much noise of ideas!
Cecity! This is it!
How good is to have cecity, sometimes!
Here, the poem is breaking! Becomes a love poem...
This silence...
Is like I know it from somewhere!
Love at the first hearing?
Dumb vertical
Make yourself horizontal like evening!
Me, the anarchist
Ran away from the fort
In Do musical note
I would like to ask
For total damage
For all unfulfilled loves!
I don't want no compensation
In dragon-flies!
Neither in Corvette!
I want my compensation in molars!
Indubitably, the old age comes
And I need at least two molars...
To still chew a piece of bread sometimes...
Eh, F.. this!
This is what I was talking about, at the shore
With Fren;u;!

THE ROAD TO YOU

The road was of water
Dust was the dawn
Behind the dreams
Paddled by love slaves...
For this imense love
It should be invented a shore
Something like
Window sill is for rain...

A BOUQUET OF...
APPLE TREE FLOWERS...

I AM GIVING YOU A BOUQUET OF APPLE TREE FLOWERS!
CATCH!
LOOK!
IT SLIPS ON THE EVENING'S BLUE SLIDE ...
THE BRIDE OF PAST DAY THREW IT AT YOU!
SMELL IT!
IT WILL LEAVE YOU PREGNANT OF IRISES AND ROSES
AND OF ROSY CHEEKS!
CATCH IT IN THE FRAME OF YOUR ARMS
AND KEEP IT IN THE MUSEUM
OF YOUR SOUL,
IN THE GALLERY
OF THE MOST BEAUTIFUL MEMORIES
TODAY I AM OBSESED!
DON'T PAY ATTENTION TO ME
OR DO!
IF YOU FEEL LIKE IT...
I FEEL LIKE THROWING
SEEDS OF DIOR PANTIES
TO GROW PLAYBOY BUNNIES...
THE TRUTH COMES OUT LIKE AN ABSCESS:
YOU ARE MARRIED!
SO WHAT? IS NO DRAMA!
IS NOT A MOVIE!
IS JUST AN HOUR GIVEN TO OURSELVES
SELFISH TO THE SQUARE!
ANOTHER KISS
BIG
AND THE BIG KISS BECOMES BIG!
AND THE BIG KISS THAT BECAME BIG
IT HAPPENS AT THE BEACH
WHAT A BEFALL!

BEGONIA GREW AND BECAME
BE AT PEACE WITH YOURSELF...
SEAS ARRIVING FROM NOWHERE
SWIMMING IN UNSEEN LIGHTS
THE FIBERS OF TENSE DAWN
TO SHAKE THE TREES IN BLOOM.
THAT'S ALL IN THIS POEM!
NOTHING, FOR THE REST!
CAMEE...
A CAME IS CALLING YOU TO PLAY OUTSIDE
OUTSIDE OF MONDANE MEANINGS
AND...
COROLLARY: BEGONIA...BEGONE WITH A DRUNK SOUL!

AB...

You'd dare to build a city
Only to keep yourself safe from the rain?
This city built out of rain
Of autumn or spring
Or of summer
From snowfalls and forgotten lightnings
From thunders and from no clouds clear skies
Is ringing to me bells like crazy
And calling from afar muses
At intersections of unrepentant thoughts!
This city perfumed with grapes
Sipped on a terrace too much in the city center
Too visible
To get drunk on love
And to float on the waves of the lips of a
highschool girl
To shipwreck
On a tooth threw over the house
In the too neighbourly childhood...
This city is my very own eyes!

DESCRIPTION OF FALLING IN LOVE

...AND THE AIR, LIKE CHILD'S SNEEZE
...AND THE BLUE SKY,
BECAUSE IT WAS GETTING DARK!
AND THE EVENING WATERFALL
NOT BLUE
BUT GOLD
LIKE A CLEAR LAKE WITH GOLDEN FISH
OVERTHREW
SPILLED
POURED
IN THIS EARTH-HAPPINESS RIVERBED.
NO!
!!
EVERYTHING STARTS WITH !!
FROM THE OPENING OF THE EYES IN THE MORNING
FIRST, THE CLEAREST,
TO THE EVENING'S PAINFUL TIME PASSING
DROP OF DEATH POURED
FROM RAINS THAT DON'T RAIN HERE...
ME- WING IN THE EVENING AIR
SUN DRAWN ON A FACE
LIKE A CHILD
WITH BLUE MARKER
FACE-PAINTING...
ME-WING IN THE SUNSET
LIKE A BLUE DEFROST
COMPACT
AND SHE-DOLL
A STILL BEAUTY
ETERNALLY YOUNG,
LIKE A RICH FIELD
LIKE THE ENTIRE SILENCE!

SURVE, LIKE A MINUTE PAST
IN CONTEMPLATION
UNDER THE BONDAGE OF THE DOLL
NO!
EVEN THIS IS NOT GOOD!
I DON'T LIKE IT! IT WASN'T LIKE THAT!
THE EVENING COAT
WAS HUNG IN THE HOOK
LOVERS RAVENOUSLY EATING TIME
THE GYPSY WAS MAKING LOLLIPOP
THE TOILET WAS GENDER MIXED
PROSTITUTE'S HAPPINESS
JAGGED VAGINA
CLAUDIA TOOK HER FOOT
FROM THE ACCELERATION PEDAL
SHE DIDN'T FEEL ANY ITCH ANYMORE

But what is rain? A sea for an hour – Ion Barbu would say, maybe..

If the sea would start in the Fall
Beyond the August's buoy,
You'd see how the silence swim,
How the treachery swims
How are brought to the shore failed exams
How distances bloom

Cut me, when the distances are blooming,
Take the index finger towards miracles
With the musical saw
Cut my musical ear
A long cut
Like a leaf fall in October

A NOTHING OF PLATINUM

It's a nothing of platinum this afternoon
A cabbage! A rag!
So you won't give it any attention.
So for this reason you'll lose it...
It's a nothing of platinum this afternoon
On which the evening will engrave with the sharpness of its passing
With the warmth of her present
Maybe a joy, maybe a regret
Not slower than the passing of a ship on this river of air...
Jelly-fish of the sea of the sunset.- Blue
Kissing the indifference of the ankles with the ankle bracelets
And the white of the ankles sprained by the indiscrete looks
Longings shaking the ships that bring the twilight
Like of some heads nodding: a No, a Yes...
I am accepting again the punishment of a silence of a playing cards castle
I kiss again the love in the country shoes and vest embroided with moon
I open a dozen of hopes and I pour it on the floor in hell...
I try a new sample of perspectives
Bug of a time, my love for you!

YOU SEE, LOVE IS LIKE TAKING CARE OF THE GRAPE VINE..

AND THOUSANDS OF NYMPHS IT SEEMS TO YOU
THAT I WATCH YOUR BIG
WRITING...
IN THOSE DAYS...OF EXITING FROM THE COLD,
WHEN YOU SLAMMED, ALREADY, NERVOUSLY, THE WINTER
DOOR,
KISSING WITH YOUR EFFORTS
THE LOGS FREED FROM THE FROST.
YOU ARE LOST
ON GREEN ROWS,
WRITTEN FROM ONE END OF THE HORIZON TO THE OTHER
OR BETTER SAID: WRITTEN CALLIGRAPHY BY RAINS AND
SUNS
FROM AN END TO THE INFINITY OF YOUR HOPES...
HERE YOU ARE VISITED BY ANGELS
AND THE SILENCE IS FRIENDS WITH THE HORSES NEIGH
THAT PULL THE PLOW
AND EVERYWHERE YOU LOOK SEE TIME
LIKE AN ACTOR DISTRIBUTED IN YOUR HAPINESS ROLE.
YOU SEE, LOVE IS LIKE TAKING CARE OF THE GRAPE
VINE...
YOU SHAKING TO EACH RAIN, YOU PROTECTING HER FROM
PESTS
YOU COVER ITS BLOOM
WITH YOUR LOOK
AND YOU ROCK IT WITH HEAD WOBBLES
AND CLEAN THE WEED
AND DIG
AND TOWARDS AUGUST YOU BRAKE THE TOO LONG VINE
ROPES

-STRINGS FOR UNINVENTED VIOLINS!-
IN THE FALL, WHEN YOU PICK THE GRAPES,
YOU RUSH TO BRING THE GIRLS TO STEPPING ON THE
GRAPES WITH THEIR FEET.
TO CRUSH THEM
AND TO DRINK GRAPE JUICE. BUT YOU DON'T GET DRUNK
YET!
IS NOT WINE YET! YOU STILL WAITING!
JUST WHEN WILL BE IN BLOOM AGAIN,
NEXT YEAR,
YOU COULD,
ONLY,
TO GET DRUNK,
IF YOU WOULD WANT TO...
AND THOUSANDS OF NYMPHS IT SEEMS TO YOU
ARE WATCHING YOUR BIG
WRITING...

MASK

Just arrived to the carnival.
It was raining
I chose a black cloak
And a Nordic mask
Maybe Celtic.
Maybe Visigothic…
You dressed as priestess of the Apollo's temple.
And I..with my hideous mask…
I approached you like a barbarian
You got so scared when you saw me
That
You screamed loudddddly
Your loud scream
Was longer than a long train
And passed much faster than the fastest train
Through all the train stations of my soul
Without stopping
On any of them…
Your long scream
Put with its power the mask on my face
So good
That I was afraid that it would stick to my skin
And I could never get rid of it…

Just arrived to the carnival.
It was raining
I chose a black cloak
And a Nordic mask
Maybe Celtic.
Maybe Visigothic…
You were dressed as priestess of the Apollo's temple.
And I..with my hideous mask…

I APPROACHED YOU LIKE A BARBARIAN
YOU GOT SO SCARED WHEN YOU SAW ME
AND YOU RAN AWAY WITH A SCARAB- WHAT AN IMBECILE
COSTUME!

BOOMERANG OF BLUE
-POETIC SYMPHONY-

MOTO:

The little ones play hide and seek
The big ones play hide and deceive

CONFESSION: TUNNEL OF WORDS TOWARDS MY SPIRIT.
FIRST CRIME THAT I SAW WAS IN THE EVENING.
THE KILLING OF THE DAY WITH A SUPREME CRUELTY.
AND I SEE OVER AND OVER AGAIN THIS CRIME AND I CANNOT DO ANYTHING FOR ANY DAY.
...I LIE TO MYSELF LIKE A FOOL THAT I SAVE THEM IN THE SOUL...
-WHEN DID YOU SEE FOR THE FIRST TIME A KILLING OF THE DAY?
-IN CHILDHOOD, AT THAT WONDERFUL AGE
WHEN I WAS READING STORIES AND EATING BISCUITS...
MY IMAGINATION WAS A FIELD FRUITING THE BLUE AND ENDLESS SKY...
WHEN THE CROCHETED VESTS OF HAPPY TO BE WERE MADE FOR ME...
-...AND YOU FELT LIKE GREUCEANU, THE FAIRYTALE HERO?
-NO! I WAS REALLY SEEING MYSELF
THROUGHOUT BEAUTIFUL EVENTS
LIKE THROUGH WINDOWS
I WAS SEEING MYSELF THROUGH A MOUNTAIN AIR, AND OF SEA
STAIN GLASS WINDOW
BROKEN BY A STONE THROWN THROUGH TIME
...THEN, THE SUNSET, LIKE A SOLAR AUTUMN...
DEFOLIATION OF THE LIGHT
DRY RAYS, FALLEN ON THINGS

Like some helpless hands
Incapable to sustain anymore
The weight of a gawky creature of a killed day
Autumn lava
Erruption of a big dramas, of a big sadness, of a
big melacholy...
-Sad...
-Yes. I loved the childhood days and I didn't want
them killed
I wanted them endless
I was sick of endlessness
Watching from the bench in front of my block of
apartments towards the horizon
and- naive- I was so happy I was neighbor with the
nothingness
That I can touch it and salute it with my gaze.
In the evening, the crime of the day, was dropping
suddenly
Like after an universal sprain of an ankle
-And? This is the story?
No!
The story is simple.
In the childhood one day I threw
A boomerang, way too far...
Before it was to return.
The boomerang which I threw when I was a kid
without knowing what exactly what it was, how
it was, how big it was,
Became an albatross drawing with his gliding
portrets of a beautiful time.
-I wonder today if the sun would be to speak
with words,
What would he say to me?
Ah, if I would understand his mimic, the blinking,
The carress with light of all things
The making of his face-
The albatross that was drawing with his flight
over the sea and earth
Became one day again a boomerang

AND HIT ME IN THE TEMPLE OF MY SOUL
NOW
I AM AT THE INTERSECTION OF CANDLELIGHT WITH THE
LIGHT OF THE SUMMER'S AFTERNOON
AND I SAY: BEYOND OF ANY EXPECTATION
THERE IS A SNOWFALL
HIT IN THE TEMPLE OF THE SOUL
NOT PAIN WAS WHAT I FELT
IT WAS A PLAIN WHAT I FELT
A SOWING FIELD
FOR SOWING EMOTIONS WITH THOUGHTS WITH INFINITY
THE UNIVERSAL ANKLE IS SPRAINED
AND THE EVENING FELL ON EARTH
LIKE A DRY BLUE LEAF
THE CHILDHOOD GROUND PLOWED BY DREAMS AND
DESIRES
WAS WAITING FOR IT ...

OF LOVE

MY LOVE.
YOU ARE A TRAIN.
A TRAIN THAT MY WORDS
NEVER CATCHES.
IN WHICH IN VAIN I TRIED TO GET ON
FROM THE TOO SLOW WALK
OF MY LOST AND WANDERING DREAM...
MY LOVE.
YOU ARE A TRAIN
ABOUT WHICH I WILL ALWAYS WONDER
WHERE DOES IT GO
WHAT DREAM LANDS IS TRAVERSING...
SUDDENLY, I AM INTERESTED IN THE RAIN'S TOURISM.
ECOLOGY OF NOTHINGNESS.
ABOUT THE ART OF GOLDEN RULES.
ABOUT TRANSHUMANCE.
ABOUT THE GALAXY OF LACES
ABOUT ADMIRATION
FROM THE TRAINS TIMETABLE I JUMP TO THE TIMETABLE
OF THE FEELINGS
MY LOVE.
WHEN I MISSED IT
I THOUGHT YOU ARE THAT TRAIN...

THE MARCHING BAND OF STOLEN KISSES

It's ringing in my head
At late hour,
In too many sunsets
The marching band of stolen kisses
Un-conducted by regrets

You can hear the muffled requiem
Of a love that could't even color the snow
Neither the cousin of a hospital salon
And unwritten white
White unsung
Unenchanted white
White unheard
White untouched...

Today I will break your acquarium
To not look at it anymore
I don't care about neither the plants in it, nor
About the fish!
I don't care about the stones brought from afar
Nor the very filtering filters...

I will also break the old windows
And I know: You'll ask me why?
You had to replace them! You had to renew them!
It's time for everything
And I know: every shard will hurt you
You will bleed seas and rivers of blood
From sprung regrets and melancholy...

And I will also kill your old horse
And the ugly and dead trees I will cut

AND WHEN YOU'LL WAKE UP CHANGED,
IN THE MORNING OF AN ANOTHER LIFE
YOU WILL SCREAM
FOR YOUR MOTHER
YOU'LL SCREAM FOR YOUR FATHER
THAT DIED A LONG TIME AGO FROM THE DEAD OF THE
OTHERS, MANY, OLD...
AND YOU'LL CRY
AH, THE REQUIEM OF YOUR LIFE THAT WASN'T ANYMORE
OF A DREAM THAT DIED UNBROKEN BY THE DAWN

IT'S RINGING IN MY HEAD,
AT LATE HOUR
-IN TOO MANY TWILIGHTS
THE MARCHING BAND OF THE STOLEN KISSES
UN-CONDUCTED BY REGRETS.

TUNED VIOLINS BY THE SPRING WIND
AND DRUMS HIT BY THE SCORCHING SUMMER
JUST ME HEARING THEM
JUST ME COLLECTING THEM BROKEN DOWN IN SOUNDS...

THEN, THE SILENCE WOULD BE A SATIRE OF A BAD MUSIC
AND OF EVERYTHING THAT WE TALKED ABOUT WEIRD
AND IDIOTIC
THEN, FOREST OF WHITE
FOREST OF DRY
FOREST OF NOTHING
AND IT DOESN'T MATTER THE SACRIFICE OF THE ONE
THAT WAS
LONG AGO. I WILL ASK YOU ONE DAY IF IT'S POSSIBLE
FOR A FOREST OF IRISES
IF IT'S POSSIBLE AZURE UNBROKEN BY PRYING LIGHTS...

AND AGAIN WILL BE HEARD IN SILENCE, THE REQUIEM
OF A LOVE THAT COULDN'T EVEN COLOR THE SNOW
NEITHER THE COUSIN OF THE HOSPITAL SALON
AND UNWRITTEN WHITE
WHITE UNSUNG

UNENCHANTED WHITE
WHITE UNHEARD
UNTOUCHED WHITE...

LOVE

Today I am not in the mood to love anymore
I release from the sentiment the kiss and will
give it to the mother sensation
Now, that I have accomplished this justice
Let me give my real caresses
Your tighs
And, your hair don't pull it up in an elastic band
I will pull it for you
I will pull it like a brunette sleigh
Your breasts are already snowed by my lips
And my breath is my soft chisel
Of your forms.

Love, I am not coming anymore today to the beach
You'll wait for me on shores like for a ship
Or like of a seagull from many that nibble from
scrap
Or like the ice cream truck
And I will not come. Like a dead man.
And this poem will not be sad.
Because the boredom killed me.

Love, today don't make me lie to you anymore
Let me be
As I'd like to be
To breeze the horizon and the wine from inside me

GOOD BYE

You are saying good-bye
And I say I'm laughing
You slap me
I pull a hair of yours
A hair from the temple
To look at you sideways

REWARD

Because I dreamt of you so much,
Today you decided to kiss me
To visit my writing
Too long, growing in time...

Today you were finally curious
To discover the calligraphy of my caresses
To read on my face the poem of the happiness that
I see you
And to touch with your lips my mouth
That was calling for you for so long...

Yes! I know that is the first and last night!
And you laugh and caress me and bite
You are playing and you will run
With all the kisses and touches of snowflakes
In my longest writings.

Today you hold the hand what wrote so much how
much that was missing you
And you smile with eyes and mouth...
And I know I won't see you again
From the veil of distance
That you will maybe appear only in the dream
That you interrupted it with... you

THE DAWN IS A TRAIN

Calligraphy of a story. White:
The snowfalls are writting on my windows
"winter".
And in the train station of the wandering looks
Enters now another color...

The dawn is a train from which want to get off
Memories. Birds. Loves. Summers. Autumns- past or
future...
What crowded vagons of blue
What a bustle in our station- ruin of a star.

The dawn is a train from which want to get off:
A warm drizzle of summer
Whispers. Caresses. Screams and days at the beach
What an insanity! How busy a minute could be.

I am making way between all that I have
To get to myself the one lost in them.
The one forgotten in their world.
In which I am just a traveler!

I run. The coffee tries to jump out of paper cup
Shuck up by my run.
What a rush to still catch a drop of harmony...
I run or I jump like a shard from the entire lens
That I was sometime
Seeing the happiness.
Once I got off the train too.
From another one. Or maybe from the same one?

I BELIEVE THAT I WILL TAKE THE SUBWAY LIKE OTHER
TIMES TOWARDS ROMANA STATION
WHERE I LOST ONCE UPON A TIME
THE BAG OF MELANCHOLY AND HAPPINESS

ON THE PLATFORM OF A MAY EVENING
FROM THE TRAIN OF A BLUE SKY
GETS OFF NOW THE FIRST STAR
I TIGHTEN THE GAZE WASHER TO GET OFF MORE
EASILY...

ALMOST WHITE, STILL BLUE

ALMOST WHITE, STILL BLUE
IS GETTING DAYLIGHT
YOU SAY HOW MUCH I LONGED FOR,
IF YOU KNOW...
I WAS WAITING FOR THIS THURSDAY LIKE A WOOLF FOR A DEER
ALMOST WHITE, STILL BLUE
IS LIGHTING UP LIKE A DREAM
AND A HORSE BREAKS FROM THE NIGHT'S SHADOWS
AND GALLOPS THE WHITE SNOWED BY THE DAWN OF THE FIELD
FROM HIM WE WILL DISMANTLE US IN THE DREAM THAT WILL COME
IN THE DEER THURSDAY OF MY WOOLF SOUL OF MINE
THAT'S ABOUT IT... FLOATING
BETWEEN
ALMOST WHITE
STILL BLUE

A HEAD TURN

YOU DON'T SEE THE SOUTHERN CROSS
YOU DON'T EVEN HAVE A GAS LAMP IN THE NIGHTS
THAT BLIND US
YOU DON'T SEE THE ALDEBARAN
NEITHER THE SIRIUS
YOU SEE
A HEAD TURN
EVERYTIME WHEN YOU LOOK AROUND
YOU HAVE A GAZE
THAT SUBORDINATES THE STARS
AND THEIR SILENCE
SAYS THAT THEY WOULD HAVE LIKED TO BE BORN ON
YOUR ZODIAC SIGN
YOU HAVE A GAZE
THAT TELLS THE COMING OF THE DAWN
YOU HAVE A GAZE
LIKE A CONSTELLATION
OF DREAMS, DESIRES, GLOW, FLICKERING, PROMISSES

SICK OF COMPARISONS

I ARRIVED
TO A WATERFALL EVENING.
I SWIMM IN TIME, WET OF BLUE,
UNDER WATERS OF TEARS

I ARRIVED IN FRONT OF YOUR FLAT
MONUMENT OF MODERN ART OF WRITING

I ARRIVED AT A SWING-EVENING
WHERE DAY AND NIGHT SWING

CHOOSE YOUR NIGHT, SHE SAID!
WOULD YOU LIKE A YELLOW NIGHT? RED? BLACK?
WHITE?

I ARRIVED AT AN EVENING
LIKE A RESURECTION
OF EX LOVES.

I ARRIVED TO AN EVENING
QUIET AS A RABBIT

PLEASE DO SOMETHING TO STOP COMPARING
MIX MY PERFUMES
TO STOP UNTANGLE THEM

PLEASE DO SOMETHING
TO STOP COMPARING MY HEART BEATS
WITH THE TIC OF THE CLOCK

MIX MY DESTINY FILES
SO THAT

I WON'T FIND ANYTHING AGAIN WHAT I BELIEVED IT IS RIGHT
THAT IT HAS TO BE, THAT IS MEANT TO BE

WHEN THE RAIN STOPPED

WHEN THE RAIN STOPPED A SEA APPEARED
AND WE WENT TO HER
AND WE WERE AFRAID THAT THE SEA WILL STOP
AND THE RAIN TO START AGAIN
AND WE WERE AFRAID FOR THE SUN OF THE MOST
BEAUTIFUL DAY TO SET
IN WHICH WE CELEBRATED THE LIBERTY AND BEAUTY
AND CRAZINESS
CUTTING THE AIR LIKE A CAKE WITH OUR KISSES
LICKING SALT FROM OUR BODIES
SITTING IN THAT SEA LIKE IN A RAIN
AND FROM THE WAVES KISSES APPEARED AND THE KISSES
CAAAAAME LIKE HIGH WAVES OF 4 AND 10 STORIES AND
US
JUST SITTING UP HIGH
AT THE LAST STORY OF THE SHINING OF THE SHELLS IN
THE SUN

SUMMER

The first drawing of the summer on the asphalt is
your shadow
Then, the second drawing of the summer
Will be my smile when I'll see you again

Then,
Dennise will paint blooming linden trees
Like some smiling faces
Of some sons
Returned
From wanderings
Home...

In the summer we'll see each other
More often and more beautiful than Narcissus in
waters!
In the summer
Our embraces-corals of the sea of air

Then, Dennise will draw the evening
And we will fall asleep embraced and kissed
On a shore of a moment stollen from mondene and
thunderous
Then, Dennise will draw the sunrise
And the sea
And we will drink coffee made with the hourglass
sand

Dennise will draw
With the eyes
Ocher and thick and thin
And red blood of Eve
Mixed with gin
Colors of destiny...

TODAY I FEEL LIKE CONFESSING

TO BE A FOUNTAIN OF TRUTH.
I FEEL LIKE YOU ALL NEED TO KNOW THE TRUTH ABOUT ME:
I WAS ADOPTED
BY A FAMILY OF WORDS
AND RAISED BY MEANINGS
WHERE THE PLAYGROUND ENDED
STARTED THE FIELD OF SEMANTICS
AND SUNS ROSE UP FROM FAIRYTALES
AND THE ROUND MOONS, MAYBE TOO ROUND
IN AN ETERNAL DANGER OF ROLLING
MY GRATITUDE GOES TOWARDS NOW
TOWARDS MOTHER AND FATHER WORD

HYMN

EVERYWHERE IS WHITE
LOOK AT THE DRYING BEDSHEETS
LOOK A SHIRT
WORN IN THE WIND
LIKE A SNOWFALL
EVERYWHERE IS WHITE
LOOK A PAPER ON WHICH I WRITE TO YOU
SOMETHING THAT WATCHED FROM AFAR
COULD RESEMBLE A BLUE RAVEN
LOOK AT THE WHITE MOON LIKE A WOMAN'S ROTULA
KNEELING ON OUR GAZE
EVERYWHERE IS WHITE
LOOK - A DIMMED BULB LIGHT
FOR OUR EVENING FACE OF THE PORTERS CARRYING THE
DELAY
EVERYWHERE IS WHITE
I SWIM IN CARELESSNESS
I FLOAT IN THE SHEEN OF SILENCE REFLECTING GLANCES
IN WHICH TEARS AND RAINS THREW THEIR ANCHORS
EVERYWHERE IS WHITE
LOOK A TROUBADOUR IN THE FOG
LIKE IS RIDING A WHITE SWAN
THE CURTAIN OF THIS POEM BE YOUR ASTONISHED GAZE
SERCHING FOR WHITE
LOOK A PAPER. DID YOU KNOW?
I HAVE THE IMPRESSION THAT I CAN BE WRITTEN

CLEAR MOONSHINE IN THE NEIBORHOOD OF MIRRORS

Let's go outside in the mirror
In the garden of our looks in love
I want to break the poppies
From the garden of your cheeks and your lips
I want to lay down on benches of kisses
Watching our glances how they pass before our souls
Let's get lost
On lines drawn with the pen of carress of the neck temples

Let's sit down
On a bench of lashes
In an eyebrow evening
Under a willow of melancholy
Watching ships floating on tears...
Ah!
Endless sadness
Boundless love!!

I miss going outside
In a mirror in which the summer sunsets that have not passed,
But on the eter's paper estranged and cold...

Touch my blue skin of late
Of an in love snake.
That I will never lose!
Running through mirror neiborhoods
To get lost in an agglomeration of epiphanies
And smiling to sit down kneeling at our secret dinner

TO SIP WITH THE MOON-SILVER SPOON
THE SOUP OF THE NIGHT...
SILENCE IN BURSTS OF LAUGH SLURPING!
AND ALL OF A SUDDEN THE WOODEN LINDEN TABLE TO BLOOM
AND ALL OF A SUDDEN THE TEETH TO LAUGH

EROS AND TANATHOS

Because in this June evening it seemed that it would snow
Laying quietly, like snowflakes.
A so called blue winter
And I decree that the feet to slide on the green and fat grass
Like some summer sleighs...

Because I cannot be the same
Decided to kill my self past:
1. The bad from yesterday- the day before yesterday.
Today, I entered in the cathedral
And cry and I worship and I ask for forgiveness
And my hand, that was hitting yesterday,
Today is caressing on the crowns and ankles is washing
Yes, I am the one that hurt you like a fool
Numeric,despicable...a pagan...
You forgive me I was wild,
That I won by losing in fact.
I am sad and alone and fallen down
And I will die
Killed by a reborn love.

WITH THE SPEED OF SILENCE

I FROZE UP AT THE COLD OF THE WORD GOOD-BYE
I TREMBLED LIKE A THIN BRANCH NEAR WINTER,
IN LONG EVENINGS OF SADNESS,
AT THE THOUGHT YOU WERE GOING TO SPEAK IT LIKE A VIPHORUS,
LIKE A SNOWFALL WITH TEETH
THAT WAS GOING TO BITE MY FLESH AND MIND.
YOU SENT ME TO THE SIBERIAS OF LONGING
WHERE WHEN IT SNOWS ON PLAINS OF NONSENSE
I WILL SEE AGAIN MY TEARS, FROZEN.
AND I WILL FALL AT EACH STEP ON THE LIQUID KNEES OF THE TEARS
AND THEY WILL FALL FROZEN ON THE KNEES OF THE SADNESS
YOU TOOK AWAY THE SUN OF YOUR GAZE.
YOU TOOK AWAY THE KISS THAT REBORN ME ALWAYS AS ANOTHER, ALWAYS HAPPIER...I AM LEAVING. MAYBE IT WAS AN ERROR TO
LET ME LOVE YOU.
IN THIS TRAIN TOO PERSONAL AND SAD AND DESERTED AND FROZEN
I LOOSE MYSELF ON A TATTERED SOFA AND SHUT UP.
AND I WALK WITH THE SPEED OF THE SILENCE. AND CRY.
AND I SWEAR TO MYSELF
I WILL NEVER PUT MY MOUTH ON A LOVE AGAIN!
TO NOT LOVE AGAIN,
IT WOULDN'T MATTER HOW DEAR ANOTHER GIRL WILL BE TO ME!
I SEE OVER THE FROZEN SEA
A FOG LIKE A HORSE RIDDEN BY AN ANGEL
RUNNING, TO SEARCH FOR A SHORE
AND FINDING ONLY ENDLESSNESS...

SOME OTHER TIME, I WALKED WITH THE ACCELERATED BLOOD OF MINE
TOWARDS BOILING SEAS
AND SAW ANGELS RIDDING
BLUE MUSTANGS OF THE DAWNS DRUNK IN LOVE.
WHEN I FELL IN LOVE WITH YOU,
I BELIEVE THAT I INVENTED THE INFINITY.
CAN YOU STILL SEE ME? FAR AWAY?
LOOK! A FIELD WAS BORN BETWEEN US.
CAN YOU STILL SEE ME?
ACCELERATED BY BLOOD
CUTTING FIELDS
ALWAYS IN TWILIGHTS OF REGRETS
WITH LIT TEARS AT WINDOW-EYES
TODAY THE MERMAID THAT LURED ME IN THE WIDE SEA OF LOVE
LEFT ME IN A CRACK OF THE TIME
MY LOVE, YOU WERE A VISUAL SYMPHONY
THAT ENDED
WITH THE MOST TRAGIC BLINK.
I AM SENSITIVE AND STUPID AND I FEEL LIKE BEATING MYSELF
THAT I FELL FROM THE HORSE THAT GAVE ME CHECKMATE!

HELL

I DON'T EVEN GET UP
AND I FALL.
WHEN I SEE YOU,
AGAIN, IN HELL...

HEAVEN

Hey buddy, you have no clue
Why I am still in heaven!
Because my Eve, coquette,
Offered the apple to Geta...

MASKS

We don't give free masks based on buddy system
Mask cost 5 lei each.
Give me change to a thousand.
If you want to see the face as well!

HAPPY SONG

1.... 2.... 3...
THE SEA WAS INVENTED FOR ME!
DON'T BE UPSET! THIS IS IT! I AM TELLING THE TRUTH.
IT DOESN'T MATTER THAT WOULD HURT YOU!
IT'S CLEAR!
THANKS, BRO'!
C'MON, BE POLITE...HE DESERVES IT..
THANK YOUUUU! MISTERRRRRR!
SO I DON'T MAKE ANY REFERENCE TO THE ANY MARINE
INVENTION! PLEASE KEEP THIS IN MIND!
THE INVENTION FOR ME IS THE BIGGEST BALCANIC
OPTION EQUIPPED WITH SUMMER
I, IN TURN, WORK HARD TO INVENT SOMETHING:
THE COOLEST LAZY SITS AND DO NOTHINGS.
THE MOST DAZZLING NUDISM- I TOLD YOU TO NOT READ
IF YOU ARE TOO SENSITIVE!-
THE MOST FROTHY SEX IN A CROWD- OUCHHHHH, HOLY
SHIT!!!!-
THE THING I LIKE THE MOST
THAT I HAVE THE CAPACITY OF TAN MY BRAIN AND MY
SOUL!
THAT IF I LAY DOWN ALL DAY AND COMPETE WITH THE
HORIZON
THE HAPPINESS BURNS ME IN FRONT OF ALL OF THEM!
TAKE IT! GET SOME!
AND HEY, WHEN I'M LAYING LIKE THAT
BETTER THAN THE HORIZON ITSELF
APPEARS JUST LIKE THAT A CHICKKKKK! HOW COOL DOES
SHE! LIKE SHE DESCENDS FROM A TREE OF SUNRAYS...
OR YOU'D SAY THAT THEY INVENTED THE LAST ROAR OF
A BOLIDE MADE OUT OF SUNLIGHT
AND SHE OPENS ITS HOOD
AND SHOWS HER LEGS AND COMES OUT OF THIS
INVENTION...

ONLY COMMODITY INVENTIONS ON THE HEAD OF OUR
WORLD, BRO!
LISTEN TO ME HOW I SHUT UP AT THE BEACH!
YOU KNOW WHY? I SHUT UP BRILLIANTLY AT SEA...
AND YOU ALSO KNOW WHY?
BECAUSE- NORMALLY THIS CONJUNCTION SHOULDN'T BE
IN POEMS!-
THE DUMBEST STUPIDITY
OF THOSE THAT YOU CAN ONLY MAKE AT THE BEACH OR
IN THE RAIN
IS TO SING!
SO KEEP IN MIND:
WHEN IT RAINS AND WHEN AT SEA,
SHUT UP!
THEY SING, BRO, THA' BEST!
THE SEA LOOKS LIKE SHE SWALLOWED THOUSANDS OF
PIANOS AND VIOLINS AND GUITARS
...OF ORCHESTRAS- I WAS SINKING IN ENUMERATION!-
AND KEEPS THEM IN HER TROAT AND SINGS WITH THEM
IN HER SEA TROAT...
AND THE RAIN? THE RAIN DIDN'T SWALLOW ANYTHING
BUT SHE HAS TALENT, BROTHER!
SHE PLAYS ANYTHING! PLAYS YOU!
LISTEN TO YOURSELF HOW YOU SOUND WHEN YOU GET
CAUGHT UP IN A SUMMER TORRENTIAL RAIN
AND SHE'S PLAYING YOU!
YOU'LL SEE HOW NICE YOU SOUND!
YOU SOUND BETTER THAN WHEN SPEAKING!
BUT WHAT IF IT RAINS AT THE BEACH? YOU SHUT UP
TWICE!
THAT'S WHY I CAME
TO THE ENDLESSNESS CONCERT
TO THE ARIA OF THE WAVES RUSTLING!
HEY, AT WHAT ARE YOU LOOKING, LIKE THAT!
LIKE THE WAVES DON'T HAVE THE RIGHT TO SPROUT
AND LEAF IN THE SPRING
IN THE SUMMER, DON'T I HAVE THE RIGHT TO LISTEN
TO THE RUSTLING OF THE LIQUID LEAVES OF MY SEA?

I DO BRO' 'CAUSE IS MY BIGGEST SPECIAL INVENTION FOR
ME BOSS
AND NOW I WALK BAREFOOT
OF MY GORGEOUS FEET
ON THE SAND OF THE SEA SHORE
AND THEN, WHEN YOU READ THESE- IF...-
I WALK BAREFOOT
OF MY CRAZY WORDS
ON THE FINE SAND OF YOUR SEA SHORE.
BRO'. AND BECAUSE THE SEA INVENTED FOR ME YOU
THINK IS YOURS TOO?
LET'S GO BECAUSE MY POEM IS ENDING
BECAUSE
YOU ARE ALL RAINED ON
WET LIKE THE SEA
AND YOU HAVE YOUR ARMS WIDE OPEN
LIKE THE SEA HAS THE ENDLESSNESS WIDE OPENED
YOU ARE, MY DEAR WITHOUT A NAME FOR THEM
ONLY FOR ME!

A SWEET GOOD-BYE

IT'S TOO LATE AND I AM LOST ON THE ROAD
AND IN THE SUNSET AND IN THE HEART IS ASH
AND I DON'T KNOW WHAT TO SAY NOW
BUT A SWEET GOOD-BYE;

I RESPECTED THE CUSTOMS OF LOVE...
THERE WERE RAINS OF SMILES, OF TEARS...
WE GOT SPOILED WITH OUR SUMMER SHINE
TO SEE, THEN, WHAT A SUAVE DECEPTIONS...

WE MET BY CHANCE, MAYBE,
AND WE WERE FOR AN INSTANT SO CLOSE
PERFUME AND VIBE I WOULD FEEL THEM SOMETIME
WHEN, AS NOW TOO, I WILL THINK OF YOU IN THE
TWILIGHT...

BETTER BE , I THINK, FOR THE DREAM TO END
TO WAKE UP, TO NOT FATTEN THE ABYSS,
BETTER TO RETREAT QUIET AND SAD,
THAN TO COMPLICATE WHAT IS WRITTEN...

REMAIN IN MY THOUGHT A BEAUTIFUL MEMORY
WOMAN WITH BIG EYES, OF A WASTING LIGHT,
BE HAPPY, SHINE IN EVERY MOMENT...
I THANK YOU FOR THAT ASTONISHMENT

LUNATIC

Aurora is the church of my eyes.
In which is worshiping with kneeling sleepy
eyelashes
To see you happy.
They watched over you all night
Like a fire
And the day will swallow their light
With which they draw the body.
You will show up
And you'll throw me a diamond
In the lake of brown eyes
A transparent circle
It will form from the water of my tears and from
its reflections.
You'll disturb again the lake of brown eyes.
On which floats, normally, peaceful a clear sky of
July.
With the rain of a single pebble.
The precious stone- eyes watching imortality
Glow blinding endlessness
Blind epic nights
From the hand of the sea brought to the shore
Recounting silences reabsorbed. Struck by the
waves like rocks

GENESIS OF A JULY RAIN

In the beginings there was a tear
From eyes like an autumn sky
Unpeeling from between the eyelids
Sliding on a lash of light
Rolling on a slidding slope of a breeze
And lost at once
On an island of fall in the sea of a summer
This sea up and down
To which I got to with my gaze in an instant
Above which no wing swims anymore
It is, maybe, the return to home of the childhood tears?
It's time for love making.
I will break the windows of your ears
With words unspeakable to children
And I will pick with my lips
The flower of your lips
It's raining
And I
Am the sentimental window sill...
This sea up and down
That touches the feet of my soul
Is, maybe, the return of the tears of the longing of home?
Ah, seraphims, archangels,
My tears are your rains
That catched you again
In worship!
Pray, seraphims and archangels
For me to not go absolutely crazy for love

AND THEN WHEN I WILL PLAY AGAIN HOPSCOTCH OF MY DESTINY
TO NOT THROW THE STONE RIGHT ON INFINITY.

POOR BALANCE

Walking
And I am not allowed to stop
I am only allowed to watch
Left and right
Not behind. That's all
In front nothing. Or everything
I can't see
I have only eyes for near
And for the skin too close
A breeze
Get's me out of balance
It's a rope
The street I'm walking
Drama, Madam
Is that we will get lost
On familiar streets
Walking towards the feelings
Because as much as we are trying to know
To calculate
To control
To invent
We will never know the distance
The nothingness
We will be lost in the distance, Madam
In nothingness
Because that cannot be taught
Excuse me, Madam
In what erogene zone do you live in?
I am in the boiling point of love

CONFESSION

Father, you told me that I am allowed to kiss her,
But you didn't tell me: son, you can get dizzy and
fall!
Father, this Eve didn't give me just an apple,
She gave me the endlessness and the thought that
without her I could die!

When it rains like at the tropics, gusty, tearing
eter,
That rain finds me just when I'm making love,
So then, on that awful storm, a barbaric feeling is
trying me:
Me to be the sky and her either earth or sea.

When we stop and the sky is clear and listening,
It appears before me
Endlessly beautiful, a sea,
Offshore with enchanting sheen, in which
Mirroring themselves, rebellious
Stars that ran away into my words...

Father, blindfold me tonight, tightly
To not see but the thought that brought me in
here!
To look at it in eyes of mine,
To scold it and to scream what a terrible
delusion!

Father, forgive me, that I was a prince ridding on
words, if you'd know...
And now I fell in a horse chase from the verb
love...
In chains of storm are dressing gaze-horizon

To stand up again longings that always to defeat
me are coming back...

Father, from my knees grew the root of this
prayer:

Teach me how to make my feelings to be my
servants!
How to quit, to forget, to forgive, to shut up, to
behave
When I feel that is too much to judge, to be
wise...

Please, tell me how to escape and how to do it
With peace my soul again to dress
I am tired, because the sleep is lost
Where can I go to look for it, to bring it back?

And my chest, Father, it's not made to keep a
storm in it
That comes from nothing, from a childish holding
hands!
He was the simple and modest house of my heart,
That, I can see now, was made from twigs...
 Of the most stinging of them...

A MEMORY

IT WAS THE FIRST EVENING SPENT AT THE WINDOW,
WHEN I WANTED TO BREAK SNOWFALL AND TO PUT IT IN
A VASE
WHEN, WILLINGLY WANDERED INTO A MUTED WONDER,
I FOUND OUT THAT SILENCES ARE SUNG.

I LEARNED, FROM THAT YEAR,
TO LISTEN HOW THE SILENCE'S SNOWFALL PLAYS AT A
WORLD'S PIANO
ON ENDLESS KEYBOARD-STREETS
WITH LONG FINGERS, OF FLAKES, SOFT AS SOME KISSES...

HOW WOULD I HAVE LIKED, NOW, TO BOTH LISTEN TO,
IF IT WOULD HAVE BEEN THE SNOWFALL-PIANO PLAYER
IN THE CITY,
CONCERT OF SILENCES FOR THE PIANO-US

LYRIC GAMES

Because we looked at each other so close
Because our eyelids almost touched
Someone found a way to braid our lashes
And us, like some romantic extensions all the way
to the ankles to braid.
Walking like that through the world! She braided
us in three: the two of us and a dream...
Because the blue eyelids of the evening
didn't have anything romantic to close
I gifted my look after you...
Don't run away from the heavy rain!
Evening at the window. 20:15. The hour when the
dough of the moon is made.
It will be kneaded by the skillful hands of the
breeze
That brings never before fallen rains.
The dough of the light needs about an hour to
rise.
Then it will be put on a round baking tray
in the oven of the desires and of dreams;
I don't know how never before
didn't come out burnt...

THIS SOUL DOESN'T STOP TALKING...LOOK AT WHAT IT SAYS...

You will reborn me
In a summer evening,
Like my mother, first time,
In an August, again, you will give birth to me!
I will come out from your embrace, from your kiss,
After nine months where I grew in your chest,
Not a child, this time, but man, even hero!
And I won't cry for breast milk, you know well
Because I'm only going to cry for you...
And I will return every evening at you
Hungry to be, to love,
I will search for you, I will call you
And I will be whole only with you

LETTER TO HER

It's not morning!
It's another continuation of the day
when I fell in love with you!
The day of mine without an ending.
I went out to jog. To run. From you. From love.
Like I could ever.
I start slowly. The cork from the side of the athletic track
Laughs tickled by the summer breeze; laugh out loud in vegetables laughs.
It's not morning. Is just the continuation of a night
When I stayed to watch the golden apples of love
-Insomnia of the prince in love and tormented
of imaginings and the fear that someone could steal you from him.
That the moon would become square, if he wouldn't polish it incessantly.
With his looks drunk in love.
It's not morning. You are dressing my eyes
With silk of light. With your light's silk.
I run. Like to get to you. You are far away.
52 laps are not enough for me to touch you today.
I am longing. I am not sad! I am happy, because I love!
I am happy!
...Is just that I realize that even she has, the happiness.
Her problems...
Like us.
I run.
It's not morning...

THE FOOL
WHO WAS WATCHING YOU...

-MY LOVE! I WHISPERED TO YOU,
WITH A HORSE SOUL BECAUSE OF THAT MUCH CRY OF
LONGING...

THE ROCKS FROM THE SEASHORE
THEY DIDN'T KNOW WHAT TO WEAR,
IN THAT DAY OF PERFECT WEATHER.
NOT EVEN THE LITTLE AND FRIENDLY ONES
THAT GOT IN THE SANDALS,
NOT EVEN THE BIG ONES THAT COULD HARDLY FIT IN
YOUR GAZE
MADE UP THEIR MINDS:
TO WEAR DRESSES OF WAVES,
OR DRESSES OF BREEZE
OR DRESSES OF SILENCE?
THEY TRIED THEM ON UNDER YOUR GAZE
KEPT CHANGING THEM, WAITING, LIKE,
TO TELL THEM WHAT TO CHOOSE
WHAT WOULD FIT THEM BEST...

THE SAME WAY, YOUR LOOK SEEMED THAT DIDN'T KNOW
WHAT TO WEAR:
SADNESS?
HAPPINESS?
WONDER?
ADMIRATION?
DESIRE?
LOVE?
I WAS WATCHING YOU CONTINUOUSLY CHANGING THEM,
TRYING THEM ON.

I DIDN'T WANT TO SHOW UP IN FRONT OF YOU

TO SURPRISE YOU WITH YOUR NAKED GAZE
AND LOOKING TO...NOWHERE...

I CONTINUED TO STAY AT A DISTANCE
HID BEHIND LONG SKIRTS. OF BREEZE AND OF WAVES AND
OF SILENCE.
OF A ROCK.
...AND I WAS JUST WHISPERING TO YOU. WITH A HOARSE
SOUL OF MUCH CRYING OF LONGING:
-LOVE! LOVE YOUR GAZE TO WEAR
IT LOOKS ON YOU BEST...

AND I GOT LOST INTO THE ENDLESS SEA IN FRONT OF
THE SEA...

FIRST ACT

IN THE EVENING,
THE BUOYS WERE TALKING ABOUT THE POSSIBILITY OF A
RAIN,
AND LOOK HOW
THE WAVES, THE YOUNGEST OF THE SEA WENT OUTSIDE
ON THE GROUND
MAKING A DETOUR
VIA THE SKY

AND THEY ARE PLAYING WITH OUR TEMPLES AND ANKLES
WITH THE LOOKS ESPECIALLY
JUMPING, DOING SOMERSAULTS OVER THE BIG AND SMALL
ROCKS
-LIQUID MONKEYS

 THIS EVENING LIKE A CURLY HAIR OF SATURN
IS HANGING FROM MY TEMPLE TOO
NOW

IT'S A KIND OF STRIKE OF MY BEING FOR THE LONGING
FOR YOU
I HAVE BEEN, RUNNING
I WAS RUNNING, BEING
AND THE LONGING FOR YOU DOESN'T GET TIRED,
INFINITE...

I AM MOVING IN A DAWN'S CAVE
NOT HAVING ANY OTHER WEAPONS
BUT THE BOW OF MY GAZE
-AMING AT YOU
 WITH ARROWS OF TEARS, NOW...

STATE

Today my time has borne fruit!
Today I will go out to the orchard of my time
At the picking!
Early morning!
Early desire!
Early dream!
In the evening,
I will stay on the shore of the day
To catch
The golden fish of the sunset.
No! I won't say what I will ask him!
He will tell me:
Ask me anything, but don't ask me to stop this
day.
Let me pass!
Screams the time in a rush
Lost
In the clutter of feelings of the dreams desires
The silence returns to me
The words I never said to you
She doesn't need them.
Take them! Maybe they'll be useful to you
someday
Maybe you'll have the courage to say them to
someone else.
I will tuck them back in my chest pocket
Of the soul
Softly, to not get them bent...

PERIOD AND FROM THE BEGINNING

Ok. Ok! Period!
I understand...but from which end to start?
From the end of the cosmos
From where you rained my gaze
First as a shooting star
Then as a sight of love
Entering the atmosphere of my life
And becoming shooting star in the embrace?

I WAS FALLING

OVER THE RAILING OF MY SOUL.
I MUST HAVE BEEN PUSHED BY THE DESTINY.
I WAS FALLING
AND WHAT A PITTY I WASN'T
SNOWFALL
OR RAIN
BUT JUST TEAR
UNSEEN
ONLY A FELT TEAR
ONLY A HOT TEAR
ON A CHEEK
WRINKLED BY LONGING

LOST IN THE GEOMETRY OF YOUR SMILE

MY SOUL EXPLODED
OR JUST I GOT LOST IN THE ROSE'S GEOMETRY
OF YOUR SMILE?
BUT I GOT LOST IN A THOUSANDS OF PIECES

WHEN IT RAINS

When the rain catches me, it's like I'm inside a vein,
The vein that takes the blood from the heart to the brain of a man in love
When it rains, it's like kids hitting their feet inside my temples
They aren't even born and they already want something!
When it rains, I hear again the foot of the young girl
Dancing Ciuleandra,
When is calm and tender,
The rain is combing the air
Is combing us, combing the trees...
You'd like to be combed with a path in the middle of the sea?
I am the rain cardiologist,
I listen to her heart beats
Sticking my ear to the mountains chest, to forests, to neighborhoods...
When it rains, Morgana eaves
Luring me on my way home...
When it rains, like thousands of kids would learn to write on the eter's paper;
When it rains, it's the sign that arrived:
The destiny of a new rainbow
To call for...?

BROKEN SILENCE

Sad? Happy?
A walk. Cișmigiu park. The place of chess players.
I am sitting at a table and write.
I can't play chess with words. To give checkmate
to the longing!
I get up like a bird almost.
A walk. The trees are the buildings of the doves.
Morning. God. Please. Make it to be morning
Not just because it can't be evening now...
Is going to rain a sifted rain through the sieve of
the clear sky
I am going to the train station. The longing is
keeping company. Urges me.
I jump in the first train.
If our life could happen in a train.
We should have train controllers of happiness. Right?
I see her. All the time.
She's in my eyes. Motionless.
Like a cherry tree in bloom. In an orchard.
Not even one blink can move or erase her.
The sleeping sponge doesn't work anymore!
I see her from head to toes.
The cigarette lighters of her ankles
Lit my longing fire.
I lift my arms to her like a fisherman's net of love
Beyond the window. Far away. In the sea of world.
The silence swims.
Beyond our said or unsaid words
I get off.
I stop from my walking
And skate
With my gaze on her tights

On her smile
I am happy

I WROTE ON THE PAPER OF THIS DAWN A POEM – 24 APRILIE 2023

With lashes in a slight weaving,
I receive your touches- tactile evenings
And your kiss of a new moon
Is cutting my horizon
With the breathing
In two...

Over the water of my words
You have risen to mirror yourself in rushed waves,
In waves of today and tomorrow
In a game of falls,
To make, in other evenings,
To fall from seas,
Not from clouds,
Only with apples,
The rains of my thirsts...

I am called by fairies
On your skin
-the slipping slide of my palms
And I run right away
With big steps of neck kisses
To have you, to taste you
Like the wine from the grape vine
That, my heart
Didn't know existed...

www.ingramcontent.com/pod-product-compliance
Lightning Source LLC
LaVergne TN
LVHW041704070526
838199LV00045B/1201